W9-BII-925

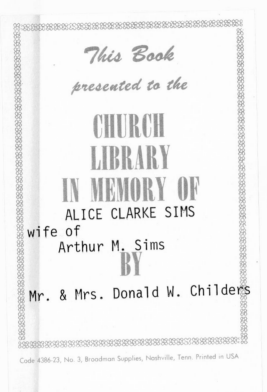

How To Face Your Fears

Is Life Really Worth Living?
What's God Been Doing All This Time?
What's New?
Does the Bible Really Work?
Is the Family Here to Stay?
Psalms for All Seasons
With Bands of Love
The Problem with Prayer Is

How To Face Your Fears

David Allan Hubbard

JUL 1983

A. J. HOLMAN COMPANY
division of J. B. Lippincott Company
Philadelphia and New York

First edition

Printed in the United States of America

U.S. Library of Congress Cataloging in Publication Data

Hubbard, David Allan
  How to face your fears.

  1. Fear.   2. Christian life—Baptist authors.
I. Title.
BV4501.2.H7   248′.4   72–5670
ISBN–0–87981–013–0
ISBN–0–87981–016–5–(pbk.)

The Scripture quotations in this publication are from the
Revised Standard Version of the Bible, copyrighted 1946
and 1952 by the Division of Christian Education of the
National Council of the Churches of Christ in the U.S.A.,
and used by permission.

How To Face Your Fears

David Allan Hubbard

JUL 1983

A. J. HOLMAN COMPANY
division of J. B. Lippincott Company
Philadelphia and New York

First edition

Printed in the United States of America

U.S. Library of Congress Cataloging in Publication Data

Hubbard, David Allan
  How to face your fears.

  1. Fear.   2. Christian life—Baptist authors.
I. Title.
BV4501.2.H7   248′.4   72–5670
ISBN–0–87981–013–0
ISBN–0–87981–016–5–(pbk.)

The Scripture quotations in this publication are from the Revised Standard Version of the Bible, copyrighted 1946 and 1952 by the Division of Christian Education of the National Council of the Churches of Christ in the U.S.A., and used by permission.

Contents

Introduction

Fear is a universal human experience. It touches us all. The newborn baby cries in fear as he faces a bright cold world, so different from the warm dark shelter he knew within his mother's womb. The weary old man in a hospital bed clutches his wife's hand in fear of what awaits him as he passes through the strange door that leads from this world to the next.

Fear at the beginning of life. Fear at the end. And in between, a thousand lurking fears disturbing our peace, distracting our energies, destroying our poise.

Not that all fear is bad. Some of it serves useful purposes. Fear of future poverty may encourage us to plan wisely and spend our money carefully. Fear of injury and pain spurs us to needed caution when we work with dangerous equipment. Fear of permanent damage and crippling disease may urge us to shun addictive drugs and sexual immorality.

In times of sharp emergency, fear shoots adrenalin through our systems and alerts our minds and nerves and muscles to be on the ready for instant action. Such fears are normal, built-in protective devices to increase our chances for survival when we walk in harm's way.

Other fears are sick. They swoop down upon us suddenly when there is no problem and make us afraid of ... we know not what. Or fears may creep up on us, sneaking in on our blind side step by step until we are gradually threatened by some dark dread that has no label. We call this anxiety. But that gives us no help in understanding where it comes from or why it seizes us.

Sometimes it is a specific experience that we fear, usually in the future. We have a way of focusing our worries on it and blowing it up out of all proportion. Tomorrow's unknown circumstances drain the joy out of today, and we live in fear—fear of failure, fear of rejection, fear of financial setback, fear of feeling insignificant, fear of temptation, persecution, and evil powers.

Then there are those subtle fears that we hardly recognize: fear of being taken advantage of, fear of not getting credit for good deeds, fear of being misled spiritually, fear of costly discipleship, fear of breaking with tradition.

And above all there are those universal, inescapable fears that darken the horizons of our humanity: fear of an unknown future and fear of death.

Human life holds lots to be afraid of. Large chapters in the biographies of all of us could be written about our fears. During the Southern California earthquake in February, 1971, hundreds of children were so thoroughly disturbed by the quake, and the tremors that followed, that they would not go to school by themselves or play outdoors as they normally did.

With fear so prevalent, so endemic in human experience, it is no wonder that the good news of the Christian gospel includes an antidote for fear. The angel who appeared to the shepherds in the fields of Bethlehem said, "Be not afraid; for behold, I bring you good news of a great joy which will come to all the people" (Luke 2: 10). Even before that, Zechariah, father of John the Baptist, captured one of the main themes of the Gospel when he recalled the promise God had given Abraham: "to grant us that we, being delivered from the hand of our enemies, might serve him without fear, in holiness and righteousness before him all the days of our life" (Luke 1:74–75).

The mysterious scene set in the fourth watch of the night symbolizes the way that Jesus ministers to our fears. The disciples' boat was being battered by wind and wave. Pulling on the oars for all they were worth, with bent backs and tense legs, they could not nudge their boat toward the shore. In the midst of their fatigue and despair they saw a ghostly figure walking on the sea. Then a familiar voice calmed their terror: "Take heart, it is I; have no fear" (Matt. 14:27).

How To Face Your Fears

Your Fear of Loneliness

15 "If you love me, you will keep my commandments. 16 And I will pray the Father, and he will give
you another Counselor, to be with you for ever,
17 even the Spirit of truth, whom the world cannot
receive, because it neither sees him nor knows him;
you know him, for he dwells with you, and will be in
you.
18 "I will not leave you desolate; I will come to you.
19 Yet a little while, and the world will see me no
more, but you will see me; because I live, you will live
also...."

—JOHN 14:15–19

A well-known movie actor put it this way: "Parties,
sex, liquor, pills—anything to get me through the night."
And a popular song makes a similar plea: "Help me make
it through the night."

Symptoms of loneliness they are, these feelings, this
song. Three billion people in our world, many of them
lonely. Tens of thousands in our cities, huddled together in apartments and tenements, in offices and fac-
tories—people crowded, yet lonely.

In some ways fear of loneliness may be worse than
loneliness itself. Being alone can be a rewarding experi-

13

ence unless we dread it. The quiet, the isolation, the privacy of solitude can do us good. It gives us opportunity to refresh ourselves from the pressures people put us under. It gives us leisure to think our thoughts, plan our lives, pray our prayers.

Being alone is part of a natural rhythm that we all need, the rhythm of involvement and withdrawal, engagement and retreat. But being alone is one thing; loneliness is another. Fear is what makes the difference. Rather than looking forward to periods of calm and quiet, we begin to dread it. Our rooms or homes, rather than being havens of security and safety, become cells of confinement and isolation. We dread the night, the holiday, the weekend, the vacation. Others live it up in fellowship and merriment, while we sit and soak in the tubs of our loneliness.

Loneliness, like any other human emotion, defies simple analysis. Certainly part of what is involved is our sense of worth. By ourselves we find it hard to believe that we count or that anyone cares. Self-doubt sets in. We place low values on our own selves. We have no one to test our key ideas with, no one to encourage us at our low points   o one to tell that we're better than we think we are.

We live by fellowship, and loneliness threatens to kill us. No wonder we fear it. And we are not alone. Jesus' men began to shudder when he talked of leaving them. Without him they hardly knew who they were. They had left everything to follow him, and without him they would have nothing left. Fear clutched at their middles

—fear of being alone, of being abandoned by the dearest friend and strongest leader they had ever known.

THE REASSURING PRESENCE OF THE HOLY SPIRIT

From the beginning, fear of loneliness has been one of our terrifying human experiences. "It is not good," God said, "that the man should be alone" (Gen. 2:18). And so it has been ever since.

Think of the tricks loneliness plays on us. It magnifies our problems, enlarges our self-doubt, exposes us to illusion. Being alone cuts us off from what we need most— someone to check with, argue against, give love to. Loneliness deceives us into thinking we are not needed. It confronts us sharply with our human limitations. It makes us even more vulnerable to frustration and despair.

All this Jesus knew as he read the fears of his friends. His response to their fear was prayer. "And I will pray the Father, and he will give you another Counselor, to be with you for ever, even the Spirit of truth, whom the world cannot receive, because it neither sees him nor knows him." Then comes the climactic promise: "I will not leave you desolate; I will come to you."

You can almost hear the sigh of relief the disciples breathed. They were not to be left as orphans. (That's what the word translated "desolate" really means.) They were to know the reassuring presence of the Holy Spirit. Christ's promise was heartening to them for several reasons.

The Holy Spirit is given by God himself. "I will pray

15

the Father, and he will give you another Counselor." The same grace and love that were at work when God sent Jesus would bring God's Spirit to them. God's program for making his love known was like a chain with three great links. First, God sent Jesus. Second, Jesus called his disciples. Third, God sent his Spirit to dwell in those disciples.

They began now to understand what was going on. For Christ to leave was as crucial to God's plans as for him to come. Their permanent companion was to be the Holy Spirit, God himself with them without the limitations of flesh and blood.

The Holy Spirit is to carry on the work of Christ. He is called "another Counselor" or "Comforter." The word "another" is key. The Greek language has two words for "another." One means "another of a different type," and one means "another of the same type." The second word is used here. The Holy Spirit is a Counselor of the *same type* as Jesus.

You can feel why the disciples were reassured. Though Christ was leaving, Someone just like him, given by God, was to take his place. They were not to stew in loneliness. They had important work to do, such as loving Christ and keeping his commandments. And now they had God's own help to do it. The counsel, comfort, guidance, and encouragement which Jesus had given while he was with them would continue. God himself had seen to it.

The Holy Spirit is able to meet all our needs. As Counselor or Comforter, he is a strong helper in times of temptation or difficulty. He gives us advice like a good lawyer and encouragement like a firm friend.

16

He is also called "the Spirit of truth." What he says we can depend on. The Scriptures that he has inspired, with their accurate accounts of God's words and ways, are entirely trustworthy. They will never mislead us. In the midst of our loneliness, God speaks through them and reminds us that he cares. And his Spirit within says "Amen" to what we read.

THE REINFORCING FELLOWSHIP OF THE CHURCH

One great work of the Holy Spirit was to form the disciples into a church. They were not to be isolated individuals struggling to maintain the faith on their own; they were to be a committed community, witnessing to God's love together.

The Holy Spirit not only brought Christ's presence to them; he brought them to each other. He was like glue that bonded them into a tight-knit group. The promise of Christ, so powerfully fulfilled at Pentecost, meant that God's presence through his Spirit would not only be with them; he would be *in them* to bind them to each other. They would not be alone. They would be members of Christ's church, pledged to one another in the fellowship of forgiveness.

To our fear of being alone, Jesus speaks two great words. He promises the reassuring presence of his Holy Spirit. And he pledges the reinforcing fellowship of his church. The Holy Spirit within us and the Christian church around us—the double answer to our loneliness. God is with us in his person and his people.

His Spirit assures us of his commitment to us. And his

17

church—the love of Christian for Christian—reinforces this assurance.

When fear of being alone threatens to catch you up, don't run from it. Face it. And hear the words of Jesus: "Take heart, it is I; have no fear." It is I who asked the Father to send his Spirit. And he did. It is I who formed my church so you could be part of a people. It is I who endured the loneliness of the cross so that my people would never really be alone again, never really cut off from God and from each other.

A friend of mine, a former student, was unsure of God's love. She felt almost rejected by him. She was not happy with herself and assumed that God felt the same. Over a period of months we talked together, and I listened to the dreary list of her shortcomings. How could God love anyone with that record of problem and failure? That was her question. "Do you think I love you, even though I know quite a bit about you? Now, don't you think God loves you at least as much as I do?" As part of Christ's church I had tried to show her God's love. Behind my care and concern she found his. And that's what really counts.

Prayer: Our loving Father, you told us in the beginning that man should not be alone. But more than telling us, you did something about it. You have given us your Son Jesus Christ and the Holy Spirit. And you have given us each other. Help us to see that loneliness is not to be our way of life but fellowship is—fellowship with you and with each other. This is your Spirit's gift and we receive it gladly. Through Jesus Christ who meets us in our loneliness we pray.

AMEN.

For further study of related themes refer to the following Scripture passages:

Matthew 28:1–10
John 7:32–36
John 14:25–31

Your Fear **II**
of Failure

[24] "Every one then who hears these words of mine and does them will be like a wise man who built his house upon the rock; [25] and the rain fell, and the floods came, and the winds blew and beat upon that house, but it did not fall, because it had been founded on the rock. [26] And every one who hears these words of mine and does not do them will be like a foolish man who built his house upon the sand; [27] and the rain fell, and the floods came, and the winds blew and beat against that house, and it fell; and great was the fall of it."

—MATTHEW 7:24–27

Go where we will, fear is apt to follow. It is our constant companion. It shadows us down the lanes and alleys of our living. With darting looks we glance over our shoulders, and it is always there.

One of its most persistent forms is fear of failure—failure in all shapes and sizes. Let our youngsters show their stubbornness for a day or two, and we parents are dogged by worry. What did I do wrong? Am I losing control? Will they ever respect me again?

Our young people have their own fears about failure.

Often we as parents give our approval only grudgingly. We are quick to scold and slow to praise. We condemn our children because they grow up at a snail's pace and then we are sorry when they finally do. Along the way we infect them with feelings of failure. "Nothing I do really pleases my mom." "How can I ever meet my dad's standards?" "My parents push me around with their unreasonable demands." "I'll never amount to anything."

At school we face fear every day. We fear we will forget when the teacher calls on us to recite. We turn in our term papers and wait anxiously for the professor's evaluation, wondering all the while whether we really covered the topic. Exams have us on pins and needles. Did we study the right stuff? Will we remember the verb endings or the dates or the formulas when the pressure is on?

The fear of failure tails us to work. It makes us worry when the other fellow gets the promotion. It turns our palms sweaty when we hear the boss' voice on the phone. It makes us extra nervous when business is slow and jobs are hard to get.

In a world where success is important, failure is a stern fate, firmly to be feared, studiedly to be avoided. And it is just here that Jesus again gives us help.

This time help comes in the form of a parable, an illustrative story full of spiritual meaning, about two men who each built a house. Storms battered both houses. One stood and one fell. The difference was not in the storms but in the building.

The difference was not in the storms. Jesus makes this

clear. The description of both storms is the same: "and the rain fell, and the floods came, and the winds blew and beat upon that house."

Jesus knew what life was like. After all he was its Lord, and it held no mystery for him. He knew that there is no way to control the storm; we can only brace ourselves against it. Take earthquakes, for instance. We cannot predict when they will occur, and we cannot lock the earth in place so that the great faults will not slip or heave. We can only build in such a way to keep damage to a minimum. A friend of mine, a distinguished engineer, inspected many tall buildings in Los Angeles after the February, 1971, earthquake. In one of them he found that cups and saucers remained undisturbed on tables on the top floor, so well did the building absorb the earthquake's jolts.

Storm sewers, storm windows, sea walls, umbrellas, overshoes, and raincoats are all symbols of our inability to do away with storms. Come they will and to all of us. Granted that some lives are hit harder than others, none of us can escape the blasts that threaten our lives with failure.

BUILD YOUR LIFE ON CHRIST AND THE BIG FAILURES WILL NOT HAPPEN

We cannot escape storms; we only build against them. At the close of his magnificent sermon delivered on the mountainside, Jesus made this point. He had taught of love, discipleship, faith, obedience. He concluded with the story of the storms and the houses: "Every one then who hears these words of mine and does them will be like a wise man who built his house upon the rock. . . . And every one who hears these words of mine and does not do them will be like a foolish man who built his house upon the sand."

House here clearly stands for life, a way of living or, as we sometimes say, life style. The life lived in obedience to Jesus stands the storms; it is built on a rock foundation. The life lived in rebellion against Jesus collapses; its sandy base is no match for the violent storms that beat upon us all.

What Jesus is describing is ultimate success and failure. From this description we learn the main point of the parable: build your life on Christ and the big failures will not happen. A collapsed house speaks of big failures, the loss of our great investments. And that is what we fear the most. Lose a few shingles, break a window or two, crack some plaster in the ceiling, and we can get along. But let our lives crumble in chaos and confusion and we are really shattered.

The failure of a life wasted is a terrifying thought. We pour our talents, time, and energies into our homes and businesses. We spend years in training and learning, and then we seek to put that training and that learning to work. We are so wrapped up in our careers that we cannot recognize ourselves without them. We are farmers, laborers, secretaries, accountants, teachers, managers, lawyers, fishermen, housewives, nurses. All good houses, these, but what are we building on? Will all our efforts be wasted in the end?

Perhaps we fear *the failure of a hope dashed*. We plan ahead, set our goals, save our money, dream our dreams

—retirement, travel, leisure, pleasure. We want to clip our coupons, visit our friends, enjoy our grandchildren, pursue our hobbies, or just rock and read. But what are we building on? Will our hopes be dashed at the end?

We should also fear *the failure of a destiny lost*. This life, important as it is and satisfying as it can be, is prologue to the next. Man lives beyond his death; "where?" and "with whom?" should be his most pressing questions. What good is a life that looks splendid on the outside and will not survive the storm of final judgment?

Build on Christ and avoid the crash. That's sound advice. No wasted life where his love has become our rule. No dashed hopes where fellowship with Christ is our goal. No lost destiny where his grace is our foundation. Let the storms come. Let hostility, frustration, rejection, disappointment blow their hardest. Lives firmly grounded on Jesus' love, anchored to his will, stabilized by his Word can take it—though they may shake and shudder some when the storms hit their peak.

Build Your Life on Christ and the Little Failures Can Be Handled

One further thought needs saying. Jesus did not promise us perfection, only stability. He does not exempt us from rocking and reeling, only from collapsing. When we build on him, ultimate failure will not happen. And when we build on him, little failures can be handled.

He offers his forgiveness. This way he keeps our house sound. Forgiveness is God's daily maintenance program by which he inspects our lives, sees our faults, and puts them in repair. In forgiveness, God does the patching.

We can no more restore storm damage ourselves than we can forestall the storms. God is the restorer, the master craftsman who makes all things new. Daily we seek his pardon. Daily he strengthens our rocky frames by his good grace.

He grants us a fresh start. Fail as we do, our failures do not doom us to keep repeating them. We may slip, but we need not be permanently trapped. God's mercy picks us up, brushes us off, and heads us on our way again.

He provides us with a new perspective. We see life differently. Paths that once looked attractive are seen as winding and worthless. Values that captured our attention are exposed as fraudulent. Causes that vied for our commitment are shown up as futile and purposeless.

This regular maintenance brings strength and wholeness to our living. "Every one then who hears these words of mine and does them will be like a wise man who built his house upon the rock." Fear of failure is part of human experience. But Christ can help us put this fear and all others into perspective. His words are the key.

He promised happiness and blessing to those who sought his will. He promised reward in heaven to those who served his Father without flash or fanfare. He commanded his own to seek God's kingdom and righteousness and to let everything else fall into place. Wise are those who believe his promises and obey his commands.

When life turns angry and seeks to huff and puff and blow your house down, remember this: In the midst of the storms stands one who lords it over all of history, even its stormy chapters. Hear his voice saying, "Take heart, it is I; have no fear." Build on me. Let your life be so solidly grounded on my grace, so firmly founded on my love, that it points its face into the teeth of the storm and dares it to do its worst.

That love and grace formed a strong cross and withstood the toughest storm on a lonely hilltop. Hatred, sin, cruelty, injustice, rejection like biting winds tried to bowl them over. But there they stood. Darkness could not intimidate them or earthquake rattle them. Love never fails, especially God's love. And that's what our lives must bank on.

Prayer: Eternal Father strong to save, we do not relish the storms that seek to put us down. But come they will. We know that. And we are glad you have made us ready. We can't believe that you would call us and guide us this far just to see our lives collapse in a worthless heap at the end. Give us the wisdom to build on Jesus Christ, who has never let anybody down. In his strong name we pray.

AMEN.

For further study of related themes refer to the following Scripture passages:

Matthew 26:69–75
Luke 6:47–49
James 1:22–25

Your Fear ▋▋▋
of Rejection

"... ³²Never since the world began has it been heard that any one opened the eyes of a man born blind. ³³If this man were not from God, he could do nothing." ³⁴They answered him, "You were born in utter sin, and would you teach us?" And they cast him out.

³⁵Jesus heard that they had cast him out, and having found him he said, "Do you believe in the Son of man?" ³⁶He answered, "And who is he, sir, that I may believe in him?" ³⁷Jesus said to him, "You have seen him, and it is he who speaks to you." ³⁸He said, "Lord, I believe"; and he worshiped him.

—JOHN 9:32–38

A terrible word, *rejection*. Few words in our whole vocabulary carry a heavier freight of pain. Few experiences in our lives cut us more sharply. Think back a moment and see how deeply etched in your memory is some event when you were turned aside, rebuffed by someone whose approval you cared about.

During my student days at Fuller Theological Seminary, I worked in a firm that manufactured parts for airplanes. My first job was at the burr bench, where I sanded the rough edges of the metal parts. Some care was needed because the parts were often both delicate and expensive. One slip with a file or buffing wheel and the part was ruined—rejected. We dropped the spoiled pieces into a scrap box marked "Rejects." They were either thrown away or sold as scrap metal.

It may be permissible to treat marred parts that way, but no person wants to be dropped into a box and labeled a reject. Yet that's what often happens when life turns its crueler side toward us. Rejection is one of our nagging fears. We may have felt it before, or we may have seen it happen to others. But either way, we don't want any part of it.

The very word "rejection" conjures up in our minds pathetic pictures. An ardent young man does all that he can to spark a flame of love within an attractive girl: flowers, notes, phone calls, repeated invitations—but all to no avail. His attention is not reciprocated and in the end he feels rejection. Or there's that classic scene so often caricatured where, with arm outstretched, an irate father sends his daughter and her small baby out into the night. Chagrined at his own failure, embarrassed among his peers, unable to forgive a mistake, he rejects his own flesh and blood.

When I think about it I can still remember how I felt when I tried out for the baseball team in high school, and that's nearly thirty years ago. When my turn to bat came, the pitcher threw three sharp curves. I waved the bat feebly at them as they went spinning by. Anxiety and tension tied me up. The coach tried to be gentle as he explained that my muscles had not caught up with my growth yet. But I still felt rejected when my name was not posted with those who had made the team.

During the past couple of years thousands of highly trained, keenly competent people have lost their jobs. Some of them had been with their companies twenty years or more. Think how they felt. Their skills and experience meant nothing. They were set aside. One can scarcely blame them for feeling rejected, even though their supervisors tried to make the transition as painless as possible.

We have good reason to fear rejection. But we also have good help as we seek to face our fear and see beyond it. Take the blind man whose story is told in John 9. Into that darkness which had held him captive from birth, Jesus came as the light of the world. But in a strange series of events the man once blind found himself rejected at the very moment when he began to see.

The Blind Man's Anguish

"And they cast him out" is the way the text puts it. The bluntness of the description matches the harshness of their attitude. Pharisees were not famous for tact or kindness, and this episode does nothing to enhance their reputation.

This flat and final rejection is the last act in a drama that becomes more incredible as the plot unfolds. At first the Jews refused to believe that the man had been born blind and had received his sight. When they found out the facts by checking with his parents, they took another tack; they tried to persuade the man not to give credit to Jesus but to praise God directly. But the man had received spiritual as well as physical sight. His answer was cogent: "If this man [Jesus] were not from God, he could do nothing."

This was more than the Pharisees could take. They had questioned his experience and discarded his witness. Now they cast him out, rejected him, cut him off from the fellowship of the synagogue with the scathing question: "You were born in utter sin, and would you teach us?"

You can imagine how the blind man felt. You can see his anguish build. All his life he had been viewed as a sinner; his blindness was his judgment. Even Jesus' disciples had thought that way at first: "Rabbi, who sinned," the disciples asked, "this man or his parents, that he was born blind?" (John 9:2). Like Job's friends, the disciples and their Jewish countrymen thought suffering was the result of sin. Rejection, therefore, was often their response to the sufferer.

But now the blind man's reproach had been lifted. Through Jesus Christ, God had brought sight and with it a whole new outlook on life. His stigma removed, the man had every right to expect full acceptance in a society that once had branded him an outcast. But instead the Pharisees compounded their foolishness by resisting the logic of the miracle: "And they cast him out."

THE SAVIOR'S ANSWER

Jesus' action was as direct and immediate as the Pharisees' rejection. "Jesus heard that they had cast him out, and having found him he said, 'Do you believe in the Son of man?'"

The Good Shepherd, who was willing even to lay down his life for his sheep (John 10:11, 15, 17–18), set out in *strong pursuit* of the outcast. An amazing note of love, this. The Son of God who had brought light to blind eyes had more than miracle-working in mind. He was not just putting on a show of power. He was committed to the total spiritual welfare of those whom he had chosen. He was bound to them with ties of care and concern: "I am the good shepherd; I know my own and my own know me, as the Father knows me and I know the Father" (John 10:14–15). The Pharisees cast out the blind man, but Jesus knew that he was one of his sheep and went to find him.

The Savior's answer to the blind man's anguish was not only strong pursuit but *straight teaching*. Experience, as dramatic as it was, could not sustain the healed man's faith permanently. It had to be shored up with understanding: understanding of who Jesus is, understanding of what Jesus demands.

Here we can let the story speak for itself. Jesus found the man and got straight to the point: " 'Do you believe in the Son of man?' He answered, 'And who is he, sir, that I may believe in him?' Jesus said to him, 'You have seen him, and it is he who speaks to you.' He said, 'Lord, I believe'; and he worshiped him.''

Appreciation of Christ's power was not enough. There must be full acknowledgment of Christ's person. Comfort brings only temporary relief from rejection. Something more is needed—a whole new outlook on the meaning of life. This Jesus began to introduce when he posed the question about the Son of man.

We need to remember Daniel's description of the Son of man if we are to get the full impact of Jesus' question, "Do you believe in the Son of man?" In chapter 7 Daniel describes a vision where four beasts, one after another, come out of the sea. They represent kingdoms, and the fourth is the most terrible of all. Daniel pictured the rulers of this fourth kingdom as horns, one of which had "eyes like the eyes of a man, and a mouth speaking great things"—that is, making pretentious claims (Dan. 7:8). Then, before Daniel's eyes, the beast with its blasphemous horn was slain by the power of God. Next Daniel's attention was turned to heaven. Let's hear about this in his own words: "I saw in the night visions, and behold, with the clouds of heaven there came one like a son of man, and he came to the Ancient of Days and was presented before him. And to him was given dominion and glory and kingdom, that all peoples, nations, and languages should serve him; his dominion is an everlasting dominion, which shall not pass away, and his kingdom one that shall not be destroyed" (Dan. 7:13–14).

The point is clear. When the kingdoms of the world have done their worst, defying God and oppressing men, God is still in command. And to the Son of man he gives dominion over all people and nations.

Here the blind man came to a deeper faith. Earlier, when the Pharisees had queried him, he said: "He is a prophet" (John 9:17). Later, his answer showed even more insight: "If this man were not from God, he could do nothing." But the climax came when Jesus found him and revealed himself as the Son of man, whom God had appointed as Lord of life and history. The man's response was exactly what this revelation demanded: "He said, 'Lord I believe,' and he worshiped him."

Faith and worship—the ultimate answers to rejection. When the King of the universe takes us in, we can put up with what other people do to us. The Son of man in all his power and glory has been our good shepherd, and no one can snatch us out of his hand (John 10:28).

Christ can turn even rejection into glory. Our blindness becomes his opportunity to make manifest the works of God (John 9:3). The blind man was rejected for being blind and rejected again for receiving his sight, a double rejection. But Christ's mighty love was more than enough to see him through. At least his rejection made him know how much he needed God. Let's waste no tears for the blind man. The real tragedy is what happens to the Pharisees. They thought they saw everything clearly and became all the more blind (John 9:40–41).

"If God is for us, who is against us?" (Rom. 8:31). This is a magnificent lesson for us to learn. Life presses against us. People react in fear or frenzy, and we get hurt. In large ways and small we feel rejected. As our little boats bob on seas churned by the winds of rejection, a mysterious figure appears in the midst of the storm, saying, "Take heart, it is I; have no fear." A blind man, brutally rejected, heard that voice and took comfort. So can we.

Prayer: Father, in a sense we are all outcasts until we come home to you. Thank you for seeking and finding. Thank you for sending your Son to be the Light for our blindness and the Good Shepherd who knows our names. We want to experience his love and power and then understand what we have experienced. Above all we want to believe and worship. For this is what life is for. In Jesus' name we pray.

AMEN.

For further study of related themes refer to the following Scripture passages:

Matthew 21:42
Mark 5:14–20
Luke 17:22–37

Your Fear   IV
of Financial Setback

^{25} "Therefore I tell you, do not be anxious about
your life, what you shall eat or what you shall drink,
nor about your body, what you shall put on. Is not
life more than food, and the body more than clothing?
^{26} Look at the birds of the air: they neither sow nor
reap nor gather into barns, and yet your heavenly
Father feeds them. Are you not of more value than
they? ^{27} And which of you by being anxious can add
one cubit to his span of life? ^{28} And why are you
anxious about clothing? Consider the lilies of the field,
how they grow; they neither toil nor spin; ^{29} yet I
tell you, even Solomon in all his glory was not arrayed
like one of these. ^{30} But if God so clothes the grass of
the field, which today is alive and tomorrow is thrown
into the oven, will he not much more clothe you, O
men of little faith? ^{31} Therefore do not be anxious,
saying, 'What shall we eat?' or 'What shall we drink?'
or 'What shall we wear?' ^{32} For the Gentiles seek all
these things; and your heavenly Father knows that
you need them all. ^{33} But seek first his kingdom and
his righteousness, and all these things shall be yours as
well. . . ."

—MATTHEW 6:25–33

Jesus spent a lot of time talking about money. A
woman lost a coin and swept out her whole house to

find it. A wealthy businessman gave varying amounts of money to his assistants and held them responsible for how they used them. A landowner paid the same wages to all his workers no matter when they started work. A foolish rich man built bigger barns, thinking he had all the time in the world to enjoy his wealth. A piece of money became Jesus' object lesson for his short sermon on our responsibilities to God and government. When money became an obstacle to discipleship, he advised the rich young ruler to sell all that he had and give it to the poor.

Jesus spent a lot of time talking about money, because money stands at the center of our living. It speaks of our need for material goods in this material world, where no one can live without food, clothing, and shelter. It speaks, too, of our temptation to become preoccupied with material things so that we end up working for them rather than their working for us.

Few things tell so much about us as persons as our attitude toward money. We can't do without it. Yet we can scarcely live with it.

If money was important in Jesus' day and became the source of a high percentage of his sermon illustrations, how much more so today. Money is the standard medium of exchange. We no longer barter, we buy. Civilization is a system of trading skills and using money as the means of trading. My trade is teaching. I teach young men and women how to understand the Old Testament. They, in turn, work as gardeners, salesmen, youth counselors to earn money to pay tuition for the instruction that I give them. I, on my part, use the money they give to buy other skills—from the farmer who grows our food, the plumber who repairs our sink, the barber who cuts my hair. The trading of skills has been greatly simplified through the use of money. Think of how hard it would be to go back to swapping job for job directly with the man whose skills you need. If he had no need for your particular trade, you would be out of luck. You would have no way to pay him if we did not have money.

Our urban society has increased our dependence on money. The yellow pages of the phone book with their compilation of classified ads are the symbol of the city. They organize the city by trades and skills and remind us that the basis of city life is that we live close to each other to take good advantage of the trade or profession that each member has.

For all its remarkable advantages, our free enterprise system has also increased our dependence on money. Wages and prices are allowed to seek their own level. Some men with huge resources and great ability are able to accumulate vast sums, while others with less opportunity or ability suffer hardship. We even fall into the trap of judging the value of persons in terms of money: he's a millionaire, she's a $20,000-a-year woman, he's just a wage-earning laborer.

Both inflation and recession are recurring threats. Many friends have written about the dire pressures of inflation. Their pensions and security checks buy less each month. Others are facing the horror of unemployment. Hardly anything erodes our sense of dignity more than to be without a job. Yet in some communities unemployment has reached 15 percent or more, and thousands of highly qualified men and women are drawing unemployment checks.

All of this breeds a certain fearfulness, especially for those of us who have long memories of bitter depression days. Part of Jesus' ministry was to speak to our fears. Nothing as basic and as common as our fear of financial setback could escape his attention. A whole section of his sermon from the mountainside focuses on this fear.

The Futility of Worry

Jesus cuts right to the heart of the issue with force and directness: "Therefore I tell you, do not be anxious about your life, what you shall eat or what you shall drink, nor about your body, what you shall put on." Worry is futile, Christ says. And then he backs his statement with a rhetorical question: "And which of you by being anxious can add one cubit to his span of life?" Some translators prefer "stature" to "span of life." But either way, Christ's point comes home. No one by worrying can prolong his life or increase his height. In other words, *worry makes no real contribution to the solving of a problem.*

Try this for an interesting exercise. Keep a daily log of all the things you have worried about for a year. At the end of the year total up the list of things you feared that did not come to pass. Chances are that the lion's share of your worrying was needless. Furthermore, even when the problems were real and not imaginary, worrying was not the best way to deal with them.

Worry, in fact, diverts our energies. It drains our vitality and skims off our emotional reserves without using them profitably. Worry may so weaken us that we don't have the nerve we need to face our real problems and settle them.

But even worse, worry is futile because it freezes our attention on ourselves. It paralyzes us into introspectiveness and distracts us from thinking about God. Whenever we leave God out of life's picture, we have good reason to worry. We cut ourselves off from his power and are left to drift without compass, sail, or rudder.

THE IMPORTANCE OF PRIORITIES

Worry is futile. That is Christ's first point in helping us to face our fear of financial setback. His second is equally pointed: *get your priorities straight.*

The person is worth more than what he eats or wears. "Is not life more than food, and the body more than clothing?" A German proverb says, "What a man eats he is." This is a forceful reminder of the importance of food and nutrition for human health, but it goes too far. It defines man in gastronomic terms. It treats him as though he were only matter, only cells to be renewed or tissue to be refurbished. Jesus did not downgrade food. He himself knew the ravishing effects of a six-week fast. He it was who fed the multitudes. But he knew that a man is a whole lot more than what he eats.

Polonius' advice to his son Laertes, who was Hamlet's friend, included words about dressing well: "apparel oft proclaims the man." Or "clothes make the man," as we sometimes hear. Jesus knew about fine clothing. His seamless garment was valuable enough to lure the Roman soldiers to gamble for it at the foot of the cross. But he also knew that God judges a man by his heart, not by his garb.

Get your priorities straight. You are worth a great deal more than what you eat or wear. Insecure as we are, we sometimes forget this. A friend of mine was raised in great poverty. In later years he earned a very comfortable living, but the stamp of those poorer days never left him. Every day after work he would drop into the supermarket and roam the aisles, gazing at the food. Usually he bought one or two items he didn't really need, just to satisfy his inner urges. Once he had no money for food; now he had plenty. But he could not rest secure with what he had. He had an emotional drive to buy fine food.

Some people feel this way about clothes. Their closets are full, yet they keep buying. Their security comes from dressing well, and they are exceedingly uncomfortable in any situation for which they don't feel properly dressed. Deep down they view themselves as clothes racks, fulfilling their purpose and gaining their dignity by displaying attractive garments. No wonder fear of financial setback gets to them. Talk of recession or lay-off ties them in knots. Food or clothes are what they live for. Eaters and dressers are what they are. Their whole existence is threatened in a time of economic upheaval. Jesus' word about priorities is vital for them. They themselves are far too important to pin their identities on food or fabric.

Our energies should be spent in doing God's will.

This, too, is part of our priority system. Worry and trust war against each other, as do anxiety and obedience. The person consumed with care about money has little vitality left over for what is really important—loving God and serving his people.

THE FAITHFULNESS OF GOD

What makes the Christian different from the non-Christian is both his knowledge of these priorities and his confidence in the faithfulness of God. Pushing God out of the scene leaves us little choice but to make the wrong things important and then worry when we don't have them. Without Christ we lose both the perspective of what we truly need and the confidence that he will fully provide.

For this reason the whole thrust of Jesus' argument is to shake us loose from our fixation on our problems and to fasten our attention on God. Feeding and clothing are what he does regularly. "Look at the birds of the air: they neither sow nor reap nor gather into barns, and yet your heavenly Father feeds them. Are you not of more value than they?" Again, "And why are you anxious about clothing? Consider the lilies of the field, how they grow; they neither toil nor spin; yet I tell you, even Solomon in all his glory was not arrayed like one of these."

God is faithful. This is Jesus' main point. Stocks may fall, jobs may be scarce, prices may skyrocket, reserves may dwindle, business decisions may prove wrong, but God's faithfulness is unchanging. Our task is to seek his kingdom and trust him to take care of our need in his own way. "But seek first his kingdom and his righteousness, and all things shall be yours as well."

James C. Penney was a friend of "The Old-Fashioned Revival Hour" and "The Joyful Sound" until his death on February 12, 1971. In 1956 he wrote an article in which he counted his spiritual treasures of more value than all his millions. Here is what he wrote.

> One night, for example, at age 56, I was broke, discouraged, ill in a sanitarium in Battle Creek, Michigan. I felt that I would never see the dawn of another day. I got up and wrote farewell letters to my wife and to my oldest son. I sealed the letters. If I did sleep, it was not a sound sleep. I rose early, went down to the mezzanine floor, and found the dining room was not open.
>
> Suddenly, over in one corner of the mezzanine, I heard the singing of gospel hymns. The song was the old favorite, "God Will Take Care of You." You can imagine how heavy my heart was when I went in. Yet I came out of that room that morning a changed man. Within just a few moments, my life was transformed. It was almost as if I had a new birth. God did take care of me. He did save me. And ever since, I have been trying to fill that obligation.
>
> When I finally got back on firm ground, I had much less in a material sense than I enjoyed before. But I had gained immeasurably in spiritual wealth, for I had learned to turn to God for guidance in all the acts and decisions of my life.

The threatening winds of economic difficulty may blow high and hard. Many of you have felt their blasts in recent months, and for some of you they are still blowing. May you, like the disciples, have ears to hear above the sound of the winds the strong, calm, friendly voice of God's Son coming as usual with good news: "Take heart, it is I; have no fear."

Prayer: Father, let your faithfulness loom lots larger than our fearfulness. You are with us, and you are for us. Does anything else ultimately count? Free us from the foolishness of double servitude. Will you please be our Master, not mammon. Make heavenly treasure our aim so that our hearts will be in heaven where you are. You we really need. Let all our other needs take second place. Through Jesus Christ we pray.

AMEN.

For further study of related themes refer to the following Scripture passages:

Luke 12:22–34
Philippians 4:4–7
I Peter 5:7

Your Fear   **V**
of Feeling Insignificant

¹ At that time the disciples came to Jesus, saying, "Who is the greatest in the kingdom of heaven?" ² And calling to him a child, he put him in the midst of them, ³ and said, "Truly, I say to you, unless you turn and become like children, you will never enter the kingdom of heaven. ⁴ Whoever humbles himself like this child, he is the greatest in the kingdom of heaven.

¹⁰ "See that you do not despise one of these little ones; for I tell you that in heaven their angels always behold the face of my Father who is in heaven. ¹² What do you think? If a man has a hundred sheep, and one of them has gone astray, does he not leave the ninety-nine on the hills and go in search of the one that went astray? ¹³ And if he finds it, truly, I say to you, he rejoices over it more than over the ninety-nine that never went astray. ¹⁴ So it is not the will of my Father who is in heaven that one of these little ones should perish. . . ."

—MATTHEW 18:1–4, 10–14

People are born small and helpless. Twenty inches long we come into the world, all eight pounds of us. Six thousand days or so it takes us to grow to full height, and we keep gaining weight long after that. At the beginning, wrapped in a small blanket, we fit in a basket. Giants with mammoth teeth, massive noses, and huge faces peer down at us. They pick us up and put us down, squeeze us and pat us. We feel very small.

We are totally helpless. All we can do is cry. Everything else has to be done for us. We have to be carried, fed, changed—and all on somebody else's terms and schedule.

Small and helpless we come into the world. Many people feel that way most of their lives. They grow physically and intellectually. They carry out their responsibilities in society, raising their families and working at their jobs. But all the while they are scared stiff inside. Their outward appearance may mark them as adults, but their inner feelings brand them as children.

The world looks tall and intimidating to them. They think of everyone as being more poised and confident than they are. In social situations they are leery and watchful, keeping an eye on people they admire to imitate their actions. When others show honor or appreciation, our timid friends are suspicious. If you really knew me, they think, you would know how inadequate and unequipped I am. In fact, you must be putting me on when you say these good things about me.

The process of growing up has left its scars all over their insides. In their own minds they are still four feet tall, nine years old, and terribly awkward. Always ready to be corrected or scolded, they move through life uneasily, fearful that their dreaded immaturity will be exposed to a laughing world.

These feelings of insignificance, with which all of us identify to some extent, often drive us in two directions. We overcompensate, or we withdraw. Either way we live in fear, not freedom.

We *overcompensate* by running hard and driving fast. We cover our feelings of insignificance by high achievements. We push our way through life, competing with everyone in sight. We may develop a brassy exterior to protect our inner tenderness. We may gesture grandly and talk loudly to mask our fearful shyness. We may become arrogant and insolent in our desperate attempt to hide what we really are.

Or we may *withdraw*. Convinced that we have nothing to contribute, we keep to ourselves. Our opinions are not worth sharing. Bright conversations tire us because our thoughts are tedious and our words dull. We find convenient excuses not to accept invitations; we back away from added responsibilities at work; we graciously decline assignments at church, knowing that almost everybody else has more talent for that job than we do.

Whether arrogant or withdrawn, we need help; the fear of feeling insignificant has crowded us into wrong reactions. For this fear and all our other fears, Jesus Christ has a good word. To both the pushy and the shy, Jesus spoke good news when he used a child as an object lesson—an object lesson of the greatness found in humility and of the true importance of every person. With Jesus' insight we can begin to cope with our feelings of insignificance.

HUMILITY IS GREATNESS

The disciples asked Jesus a question that showed them itchy with ambition: "Who is the greatest in the kingdom of heaven?" Not an academic question, this, but a purposeful one. The disciples had hoped to be among the greatest in the kingdom. The desire for power and recognition burned bright within them as it does in many of us. They wanted God's approval and the sense of satisfaction that comes with it. Jesus' talk of kingdom, power, and glory was too much for them. It went to their heads. These fishermen, tax collectors, and laboring men were thirsty to share in all of this. And they wanted to know how they ranked.

Jesus' answer to the disciples' ambitious question about greatness in the kingdom came in the form of a pointed object lesson. "And calling to him a child, he put him in the midst of them, and said, 'Truly, I say to you, unless you turn and become like children, you will never enter the kingdom of heaven. Whoever humbles himself like this child, he is the greatest in the kingdom of heaven.' "

Humility is greatness—that was Jesus' answer. You can imagine how it splashed like ice water over the disciples' hot aspirations. They were ready to present other credentials: knowledge of God's ways, skill in leadership, power in prayer. Christ taught otherwise. The most important thing about God's kingdom is that it is God who is King. He is not impressed by our achievements, but he does accept us in our humility.

The more confident and self-reliant we are, the harder humility is to come by. The two verbs Jesus used

47

show this: "unless you turn and become like children, you will never enter the kingdom of heaven." *Turn* and *become*.

Turn is the word of conversion. It shows how foreign true humility is to our way of life. Our fears and insecurities trick us so that we deceive ourselves and others into thinking we are more important than we are. White with inner fright, we pretend to be confident. Wobbly with fear, we try to steady ourselves with pride and haughtiness. We have to turn, to change, to reverse ourselves and begin to trust in God.

If *turn* is the verb of conversion, *become* is the word of authenticity. Mock humility is no solution to our driving self-assertion, our flagrant insolence. No thin veneer of modesty can cover cracks that run so deep. We are to become like children, humbly trusting, fully dependent. Humility is greatness as God measures it. And it is his measurement that matters most.

PERSONS ARE IMPORTANT

The second part of Jesus' object lesson speaks particularly to those whose feelings of insecurity have scared them into withdrawing. Remember what Jesus did: "And calling to him a child, he put him in the midst of them." Nothing is said about the child—no name, no family line, no place of origin. Just a child.

There's a message here that is not to be missed. The child was not selected for his intellectual prowess, his physical attractiveness, his athletic aptitude, his distinguished lineage. He was chosen because he was important as a person, not because of potential or accomplishment.

We are apt to lean down to young children, pat them patronizingly on their heads, and ask, "What are you going to be when you grow up?" We mean well, but we don't grasp the implication of the question. We are actually suggesting that children have no being, no worth, no significance until they grow up and do something.

How different is Jesus' attitude. Let the shy, underconfident, self-depreciating friends among us hear him. No one—not even children or those who still feel inadequate like children—no one is unimportant to Christ. "See that you do not despise one of these little ones; for I tell you that in heaven their angels always behold the face of my Father who is in heaven." Think of it, little children have high priority in heaven, guarded by the angels close to the throne of God. If children are so well regarded in heaven, where God's will is always done, how should we treat them on earth? As persons, important not for what they have achieved but for what they are, made and loved by God.

These little ones whom we are apt to ignore or exploit are not only watched by the angels; they are sought by God. This is the point of Jesus' parable of the ninety-nine sheep left on the hills by the shepherd while he moves out to find one stray. "And if he finds it, truly, I say to you, he rejoices over it more than over the ninety-nine that never went astray." God takes joy in the rescue of these little ones: "So it is not the will of my Father who is in heaven that one of these little ones should perish."

Two conclusions follow from what we have said.

First, *our true significance comes from our relationship to God.* This is hard to believe because our society attaches so much importance to other values. "He's a brilliant conversationalist"; "she's an accomplished musician"; "he's a successful banker"; "they have a charming home." Values like these rank so high that those who fall short of them often feel out of it. But to be related to God, to be part of his kingdom, is worth everything. The only ultimate dignity in life comes from belonging to God's family. Our true significance comes from our relationship to him.

The second conclusion is that *our relationship with God hinges on our childlike trust.* Any other basis for relationship will crumble, because it fails to reckon with who God is. If we see ourselves any other way than as children who can live only by his help and grace, we miss the meaning of life. God is unimpressed by our accomplishments; God has no need of our possessions. He does want us simply to depend on him, or better still to recognize that we do depend on him.

Feelings of insecurity? Sure we have them. But we don't have to let them lure us into overcompensating. Nor do we want to let them cut us off from full membership in the human family. Neither building ourselves up nor cutting ourselves down, neither pushing forward nor hanging back is the best answer. Trust in God is.

When fear of insignificance threatens to swamp your boat and dump you in the drink, remember those strong sounds that pierced the storm: "Take heart, it is I; have no fear."

Venture on him, venture wholly;
Let no other trust intrude.
None but Jesus, none but Jesus,
Can do helpless sinners good.

Prayer: To call you Father is not hard; but to turn and become little children is. All our lives we have been told to grow up. Now Jesus tells us to grow young. Forgive us both our false pride and our mock humility. Write your values of love and trust deep on our hearts. The only success we really want is to be successful servants of yours. Make us such for Jesus' sake.

AMEN.

For further study of related themes refer to the following Scripture passages:

Matthew 6:25–33
Mark 9:33–37
Luke 9:46–48; 15:3–7

Your Fear of Being Defeated by Evil

VI

¹ Then Jesus was led up by the Spirit into the wilderness to be tempted by the devil. ² And he fasted forty days and forty nights, and afterward he was hungry. ³ And the tempter came and said to him, "If you are the Son of God, command these stones to become loaves of bread." ⁴ But he answered, "It is written, 'Man shall not live by bread alone, but by every word that proceeds from the mouth of God.'" ⁵ Then the devil took him to the holy city, and set him on the pinnacle of the temple, ⁶ and said to him, "If you are the Son of God, throw yourself down; for it is written, 'He will give his angels charge of you,' and 'On their hands they will bear you up, lest you strike your foot against a stone.'" ⁷ Jesus said to him, "Again it is written, 'You shall not tempt the Lord your God.'" ⁸ Again, the devil took him to a very high mountain, and showed him all the kingdoms of the world and the glory of them; ⁹ and he said to him, "All these I will give you, if you will fall down and worship me." ¹⁰ Then Jesus said to him, "Begone, Satan! for it is written, 'You shall worship the Lord your God and him only shall you serve.'" ¹¹ Then the devil left him, and behold, angels came and ministered to him.

—MATTHEW 4:1–11

Fear stalks our city streets. Warily men and women edge along in unfamiliar places. Nervously on guard, they watch for suspicious moves or menacing gestures. In some large cities there are sections where taxi drivers will not venture after dark, where couples will not stroll through parks at dusk, where little children no longer use the public playgrounds.

Evil is so rampant, crime is so rife, lawlessness is so flagrant that much of the time we do not feel safe. We organize our neighborhoods into block patrols to protect our school children. We carry insurance against theft and burglary. We label our possessions for ready identification if they are stolen. We put bolts and chains on our doors to reinforce their locks. The phone numbers for police and sheriff are close at hand. We are afraid.

A pastor of a church in one of our great cities told me that 75 percent of the older people in his congregation had been accosted or held up on the street during the past three years. Deliberately they carry only three or four dollars when they go out alone. If they carry no money, they are in grave danger of being hurt by a frustrated bandit. If they carry larger sums of money, sooner or later they are sure to be robbed.

This is a deplorable situation, one that calls for concerted action among responsible citizens and government agencies. A deeper commitment to law and justice is necessary, together with a pressing concern for dealing with the poverty and bigotry and oppression which add such volatile fuel to the fires of crime.

As frightening as the evil around us is, we must not allow it to divert our attention from the potential for evil that lies within us. Jesus once talked to his countrymen about this: "Hear me, all of you, and understand: there is nothing outside a man which by going into him can defile him; but the things which come out of a man are what defile him" (Mark 7:14–16). Then later, to his disciples, he explained what he meant. "Do you not see that whatever goes into a man from outside cannot defile him, since it enters, not his heart but his stomach, and so passes on? . . . What comes out of a man is what defiles a man. For from within, out of the heart of man, come evil thoughts, fornication, theft, murder, adultery, coveting, wickedness, deceit, licentiousness, envy, slander, pride, foolishness. All these evil things come from within, and they defile a man" (Mark 7:18–23).

One reason the evil around us is so frightening is that it reminds us of the dire possibilities of evil within us. The morning paper and the evening newscast are not only cameras which snap pictures of the devilish things that go on in our society. They also can be mirrors which reflect the angry attitudes, the sick desires, the selfish motives we know to lurk inside ourselves.

It is Jesus' long list of crimes against ourselves that down deep we fear—evil thoughts, fornication, theft, murder, adultery, coveting, wickedness, deceit, licentiousness, envy, slander, pride, foolishness. Not a pretty list but a true one. Of course not everyone is tempted in all of these areas every day. But when we really face ourselves, we know that in one of these sins or another we are never far from disaster. And the person who thinks that none of these evils could ever overtake him is in the gravest danger of all.

Man's history of dealing with temptation is not a heroic one. He lost the battle without much struggle in the beginning and has been losing with marked regularity ever since. Small wonder, then, that one of our great fears is the fear of being defeated by evil. We have all had the experience of the little girl I heard about. She was having trouble with temptation, disobeying her mother by taking cookies between meals. Her mother told her that the next time she was tempted she should say, "Get thee behind me, Satan!" When her mother discovered more cookies missing, she asked her daughter what had happened. The little girl's eyes grew large as she explained the situation to her mother. "You see, I was standing by the cookie jar, tempted to put my hand in. I told Satan to get behind me, and you know what? He pushed my hand right in that cookie jar."

One of the things that we secretly fear is that when Satan starts to push us to do wrong we will cooperate readily. But it does not have to be this way. With Jesus' good help this fear, like all others, can be faced.

THE MANY FACETS OF EVIL

Jesus' comfort is especially effective in temptation, because he knows so much about it at first hand. From the desert beyond Jordan at the beginning of his ministry to the garden of Gethsemane at its close, temptation was his constant companion. The author of Hebrews has encouraging words just at this point. "For because he himself [Jesus] has suffered and been

tempted, he is able to help those who are tempted"
(Heb. 2:18).

No one knows the many facets of evil better than
Jesus. His forty days alone in the wilderness put him to
the test in every possible way. To the lure of temptation he was no stranger. With the odds stacked against
him he faced three great attacks and came off the winner. The three great styles of temptation with which
the world tries to seduce all human beings were brought
to bear on him—"the lust of the flesh and the lust of
the eyes and the pride of life" (I John 2:16).

For nearly six weeks Jesus fasted. Then, hungry to
the bottom of his being, he heard the proposition of
the tempter: "If you are the Son of God, command
these stones to become loaves of bread." Jesus had the
power, make no mistake about it. But to use that power
would have cut him off from us. We don't have divine power; we are not eternal sons of God, divine
persons in human nature as he was. One of Christ's
greatest acts of love took place when he deliberately,
gladly limited himself to our human circumstances, refusing to call on his own power but depending completely on his Father. As important as bread may be, it is
not the true staff of life. The word of God is. "Man shall
not live by bread alone, but by every word that proceeds from the mouth of God."

When Jesus refused to succumb to the lust of the
flesh, hungry though he was, the tempter turned to
the pride of life. You have demonstrated your firm
trust in God's word, Satan argued. Now, prove that
you really believe God by throwing yourself down

from the temple's pinnacle, trusting God to rescue you as he has promised.

What a story that would make. The headlines would scream, Carpenter of Nazareth Rescued by Divine Power from Deadly Fall. Jesus would have been a celebrity, his autograph a collector's item. All this Jesus rejected. His task was to do God's will, not to enhance his own reputation. Pride had been man's downfall in the beginning, and it could play no part in the mood of the man who came to make up for the first man's mistakes.

Satan's final appeal was to the lust of the eyes. "All the kingdoms of the world and the glory of them" he showed Jesus from the top of a high mountain. Jesus came to be King of kings. The kingdoms that he saw would one day be his. He wanted them, but not at Satan's price. As much as his eyes found them attractive, his heart said *no*.

The lure of the temptations and the skill of the tempter combine to show us how many-sided evil is, and how much to be feared. Look again at Satan's strategy. He began by hitting Christ at his weak point—ravaging hunger. The Master could almost taste the bread he was tempted to make. When Christ parried the thrust at his weak spot, Satan attacked his strength—his trust in God. Prove it, Satan chided. Show the whole countryside how great your trust in God really is. Jump. The world will cheer your dramatic rescue.

A further ploy of Satan was to turn Christ's weapon against him. Jesus quoted Scripture, and the devil quoted Scripture right back at him. Christ said, "It is written."

Satan answered, You're right. Now let me tell you what else is written.

THE ONE SURE DEFENSE

The triple temptation and the ample skills of the tempter are met head on by the one sure defense, the Word of God. No divine credentials are flashed, no miraculous power is invoked. The Word of God is simply quoted. "It is written" is Christ's armory.

How do we face our fears, especially our fear of being defeated by evil? The same way Jesus did—in the power of God's Word.

God's Word works when we face temptation because it protects us against insolence. The worst sin of all, the greatest weakness we are prone to, is to think that we can resist temptation on our own. Without God's Word we can scarcely tell good from evil, right from wrong, blessing from hurt. We cannot, we dare not, face the temptation that lies around us or the evil that lurks within us without the protection of God's Word.

When we use the Bible to ward off temptation we also affirm God's authority. We remind ourselves and the tempter of Who is really in charge. Pushy and clever as Satan is, he would like us to believe that he is unbeatable, that his power is unlimited, that his triumph is inevitable. Not so, the Bible says, and lays bare the devil's lie. The Book of Job, for instance, shows Satan for what he is: a rebellious creature of God with craft and power but—and this is the main point—completely subservient to God. What Satan does to Job he has

God's permission to do. Beyond God's limits, Satan can not go.

Three lessons which help us face our fears should not be missed in Jesus' three temptations. First, *the lesson of priority*. Food is important, but more important is hearing God's voice and responding to it. For us as for Jesus, evil may consist of preferring something good to the will of God. The lesson of priority is that anything, however good it may seem, must be set aside if it hinders God's will in our lives.

Second is *the lesson of purpose*. The love and power, the care and concern which God shows are for his purposes, not for ours. We are not to put God to the test by foolishness or rashness. God is building a kingdom, not running a circus. He calls us to be faithful disciples, not flashy stunt men. Our aim is not to be as wild as we dare but to be as obedient as he wills.

The lesson of patience is the third. Christ will get his kingdoms, but in God's time and in God's way. An obedient life, a submissive death, a startling resurrection, and a glorious return to earth are what it takes. The means are as important as the end. No shortcuts are allowed.

Take another look at what's frightening you. Christ's temptation can bring it into perspective. His victory can trim your fear down to size. Don't be overwhelmed by how bad you are. Rejoice, instead, in how powerful God's help can be.

The voice that put down the tempter in the desert also lifted up the spirits of his disciples when the seas ran contrary and the winds were high: "Take heart, it is I; have no fear." These were Jesus' words to them. What is he saying to you?

Prayer: Thank you, Father, for Jesus' example. Teach us to find our strength where he found his— in your Word. Thank you, too, for Jesus' understanding. Remind us that, in whatever temptation we find ourselves, Jesus has been there first and knows how strong it is. Thank you, especially, for Jesus' forgiveness. Comfort us with it when temptation gets the upper hand. May your last words not be of our problems and failure but of your love and power. In Jesus' name we pray.

AMEN.

For further study of related themes refer to the following Scripture passages:

Deuteronomy 6:16; 8:3
Psalm 91:11–12
Luke 4:1–13

Your Fear
of Being Persecuted

VII

¹⁰ "Blessed are those who are persecuted for righteousness' sake, for theirs is the kingdom of heaven.

¹¹ "Blessed are you when men revile you and persecute you and utter all kinds of evil against you falsely on my account. ¹² Rejoice and be glad, for your reward is great in heaven, for so men persecuted the prophets who were before you.

²⁸ And do not fear those who kill the body but cannot kill the soul; rather fear him who can destroy both soul and body in hell. ²⁹ Are not two sparrows sold for a penny? And not one of them will fall to the ground without your Father's will. ³⁰ But even the hairs of your head are all numbered. ³¹ Fear not, therefore; you are of more value than many sparrows. ³² So every one who acknowledges me before men, I also will acknowledge before my Father who is in heaven; ³³ but whoever denies me before men, I also will deny before my Father who is in heaven. . . ."
—MATTHEW 5:10–12; 10:28–33

Most of us are strangers to persecution. We live in cultures where religious tolerance is a way of life. Our governments protect our freedom to worship how and where we choose. We can label ourselves Baptist, Presbyterian, Pentecostal, Catholic, without fear of hostility or defamation.

Rarely would our homes be pelted with vegetables or our youngsters insulted on the way to school because of opposition to our religious beliefs. Our societies are pluralistic. People of widely divergent points of view in religion and politics live side by side, usually with some degree of friendliness.

This scarcity of persecution in parts of the world where most of us live is, to some degree, a tribute to the impact of the Christian gospel. The civilizing effect of its message of love and concern, of human dignity and divine grace, has left its mark all over us whether we know it or not.

But this picture of peace and tolerance is only part of the story. Persecution has had a long and continuous history in the life of the church around the world. Like a scarlet cord it wends its bloody way through the centuries and across the continents. From the Sanhedrin that imprisoned Peter for his preaching to the Cominform that presses young people to join the Party, partisan groups or powerful governments have persecuted Christians. And unfortunately at times Christians have been the persecutors, during the crusades and the Spanish inquisition, for instance.

Right now in many places around the world Christians are under fire. In African villages, in Latin American barrios, among New Guinea tribes, and behind iron and bamboo curtains, people who are open about their faith in Jesus Christ may be called to pay a price—rejection, abuse, economic pressure, physical harm. As members of the body of Christ we are all involved in the persecution. When other Christians bleed, we hurt. They are part of us and we of them. Hear Paul's word: "If one member suffers, all suffer together" (I Cor. 12:26).

But in less dramatic forms we may know persecution right where we are. People who take strong stands for righteousness in their communities or on their jobs may feel the bite of sharp opposition. This persecution can take many forms. Sometimes it is violent. Pastors and laymen who work for righteous reforms in their neighborhood often receive threatening phone calls and hostile notes from those who oppose them. Not too long ago a pastor in a ghetto area told me that he left his phone off the hook for two weeks because of menacing messages from men who hate the cause of Christ.

Buck the status quo, stand up for your convictions, criticize the foolish beliefs or the false values embraced by those around you, and persecution may follow. You may not be burned at the stake or slapped into some dark dungeon, but you may be shunned by those you'd like to help. You may be put down by those you'd like to build up.

The fear that this may happen often freezes us into silence and inactivity. Our emotions become a swirl of ambivalence. We resent the opposition that muffles our Christian witness, and we deplore the cowardice that keeps us from witnessing anyway. We feel resentful of others and disappointed in ourselves—a frightful predicament, yet all too common.

TEST WHAT IS HAPPENING

If fear of opposition, criticism, persecution keeps us from being God's bold people, we have to find help to face this fear. Some basic questions need to be asked when we begin to feel persecuted. The first question is, *Am I really being persecuted?* This sounds silly until we remember that feeling persecuted and being persecuted are not necessarily the same thing. Christ's promise is: "Blessed are those who are persecuted for righteousness' sake, for theirs is the kingdom of heaven." He makes no similar pledge to those who suffer from persecution complexes.

The human psyche plays strange tricks on us at times. Someone looks at us strangely, and we suspect a plot. Two people whisper when we enter the room, and we detect a conspiracy. Our plans fall through, and we are sure someone has sabotaged them. Once this suspicion begins to fester we misread everything else that goes on.

That's why we need to test what's happening when we feel persecuted. We need to check these feelings with others to get their perspective. We may even want to talk with those who seem to be criticizing us to determine their true feelings. Persecution is one thing; paranoid feelings are another. Sometimes we need help to tell them apart.

Am I really being persecuted? That's the first question. If we examine the situation as objectively as possible and come to an affirmative answer, we have a second question to put to ourselves: *Why am I being persecuted?*

Self-righteousness comes easily to all of us. This means that criticism or opposition is hard to take. But we will be more stupid than we need to be if we don't learn from our opponents. Sometimes their criticisms are valid, and we should listen to them. This ties in with Jesus' note on blessing: "Blessed are you when men revile you and persecute you and utter all kinds of evil against you falsely on my account." *Falsely* is the word to focus on here. Blessing may come from true criticism if we pay attention to it and mend our ways. But we cannot apply this hopeful promise unless we are being judged falsely. That's another reason why we have to test what is happening.

Persecution is always painful. But Jesus' point has to do with its purpose, not its pain. Two phrases make this clear—"for righteousness' sake" and "on my account." This is a specific kind of suffering that Jesus has in mind. This cruel world of ours is full of hurts. Browse through the daily newspaper in any large city; the evidence is all there: murder, robbery, assault, rape, extortion, embezzlement, libel, slander, malpractice. These and other crimes are the daily diet of city dwellers. Christian and non-Christian alike may be the victims. But the purpose of the crime may not be persecution at all. Greed, lust, malice, hostility may be involved. What Jesus talks about, however, are the times when people deliberately attack or accuse Christians because of what they do or say as Christians.

TRUST YOUR HEAVENLY FATHER

Not everything bad that happens to us is really persecution for Christ's sake. That's why we test what is happening. Well then, what if we find that we are really being criticized or opposed because of our Christian faith? Trust your heavenly Father. That's Christ's firm advice.

Trust in God is especially needed when things go wrong. Here we are confronted with the radical nature of this promise. Blessing and persecution we consider as opposites—mutually exclusive experiences. This was the pattern through most of the Old Testament. When the people of Israel pleased God, they were blessed with peace and prosperity. When they wavered in their worship or wandered from his will, judgment was the inevitable result. The book of Judges is a lengthy mural whose design is to illustrate this point. The pattern became so ingrained that, whenever anyone suffered, his friends suspected sin as the cause. The friends of Job believed so firmly that suffering was always the result of sin that they spent more than twenty chapters trying to persuade Job to repent.

But Jesus says this pattern is broken. Out of persecution can come happiness because God is at work. He can be trusted to work his will despite persecution. His kingdom will come no matter what obstacles sinful men try to throw on the tracks to derail it. That's why he can guarantee a place in his kingdom to anyone who is persecuted for Christ's sake.

A friend of mine lost his job not long ago. He and his boss had a basic conflict over a definition of honesty. The boss wanted my friend to make false statements about the product they were manufacturing. In all good Christian conscience my friend could not make those statements. When he refused, he was fired—persecuted for righteousness' sake. Yet God was with him and provided another opportunity in a business that has grown beyond belief. Blessing from persecution—the blessing of a clear conscience and the blessing of divine provision.

"Rejoice and be glad." This is our response to persecution. These words bring us face to face with the reassuring nature of this promise. The reassurance is twofold: we will be rewarded in heaven; we will follow in the train of the great prophets. These two statements give us perspective to deal with persecution, and this perspective helps stamp out fear.

"Rejoice and be glad, for your reward is great in heaven." A reminder this is that God's evaluation of our lives is what really counts. When others put us down we can easily be discouraged or tempted to compromise. But that heavenly prospect, God's approval, keeps us steady. And so does the reassuring thought that some of God's best servants have walked the way of persecution: "for so men persecuted the prophets who were before you."

Out of persecution for righteousness' sake, blessing will come. Therefore, we need not fear. Our ability to take whatever opposition and hostility and criticism people hurl against us is part of God's plan for making his name known in the world. Our steadiness in trial becomes proof of our sincerity and evidence of God's provision.

We know what Christians have been through in the past—at the hands of hostile bigots, savage tribes, pagan emperors. We will want to be ready for anything the future holds. Some of the church's finest hours have been lived in persecution and may be once again. Meanwhile, let's be prepared for whatever comes, firm in our convictions, assured in our faith. A colleague of mine at Fuller Theological Seminary knows at first hand what it is to be persecuted for Christ's sake: his family threatened, his ministry maligned, his home attacked, his life in jeopardy. He stood up for his conviction that Christian fellowship cannot be restricted to people of any one racial group. And the opposition to his stand turned bitter. He put God's promise to the test and found it to be true. In the midst of persecution came blessing.

The disciples on that stormy night thought that the full anger of the universe itself was unleashed against them. Then they spied that silhouette and heard that commanding voice: "Take heart, it is I; have no fear." Let all whose faith is proving costly, whose values are under fire, whose convictions are being criticized hear that voice calling in the night. And let them put their fears to rest.

> Prayer: Father, we are not asking for persecution. How and when it comes we leave to you. But please don't let fear of it back us away from what we believe. Hold us steady as you did prophets and apostles and keep us rejoicing even when we do not seem to have good reason for it. From his cross Jesus certainly showed us how. And it is in his name that we pray.
>
> AMEN.

For further study of related themes refer to the following Scripture passages:

II Chronicles 36:16
James 5:10–11
I Peter 3:14, 4:14

⁷ Jesus withdrew with his disciples to the sea, and a great multitude from Galilee followed; also from Judea ⁸ and Jerusalem and Iduméa and from beyond the Jordan and from about Tyre and Sidon a great multitude, hearing all that he did, came to him. ⁹ And he told his disciples to have a boat ready for him because of the crowd, lest they should crush him; ¹⁰ for he had healed many, so that all who had diseases pressed upon him to touch him. ¹¹ And whenever the unclean spirits beheld him, they fell down before him and cried out, "You are the Son of God." ¹² And he strictly ordered them not to make him known.

—MARK 3:7–12

There are two kinds of people whom Satan likes: people who pay no attention to him and people who think about him most of the time. C. S. Lewis taught us this years ago in his *Screwtape Letters*, and nothing since has happened to prove him wrong.

Not that Satan, with his capacity for deceit and destruction, with his inbuilt enmity toward God and all that's good, can really like anybody. What I mean is that these two kinds of people play into his hostile hands.

Our society harbors many examples of both kinds.

One form of the argument goes: Who would be so brash, so medieval, as to talk about Satanic power in our enlightened age? Oh, Dante and Milton with their grim pictures of Lucifer and his fallen hosts make quaint literature. But no *modern* man can take their existence seriously. After all, the devil and his demons are just an antiquated way of accounting for a lot that's wrong in life. Accident, calamity, ill fortune, moral wickedness should not be blamed on a good and loving God, so the troops of Satan became convenient scapegoats.

Bizarre behavior that once was blamed on demons was just the result of chemical imbalance or childhood emotional upsets. Medicine and psychology now give us clearer explanations and better solutions to these problems. So sophisticated modern man believes.

And all the while Satan chortles. Secure in his strategy, confident in his approach, he proceeds to deceive man and rob him of his beliefs, values, and dignity. The grand enemy delights in those who doubt his existence. Their doubt makes them so much easier to deal with.

On the other end of the spectrum, yet equally gullible, are those who become preoccupied with the powers of evil. Fascinated at times and fearful at others, they fix their attention so steadily on Satan's works and wiles that they lose sight of God.

They take the existence of evil seriously, all right, so seriously that they are almost hypnotized. I once knew an elderly Christian woman who spent much more time rebuking demons in her prayers than praising Christ. The terror of evil was more real to her than the power of God. I can hear some of her prayers now, and I have not seen her for twenty-five years. The anxiety and anguish with which she faced life stick in my memory. She seemed empty of joy, devoid of peace. Her constant attention to Satan and his forces had looted her of zest and nearly of sanity.

Granted, her situation was extreme, yet our generation contains a fair sampling of people who are over-occupied with the power of evil. There are many reasons for this.

For one thing, interest in occult and mystical religions is probably higher now than at any time in our century. Witchcraft, sorcery, and spiritism command a great deal more attention than one would anticipate in a scientific age. Almost every university campus has at its edge a bookstore that specializes in books that deal with magic and the spirit world. Both the quest for meaning and the rebellion against authority have contributed to this rage. Young people want to investigate new paths that hold promise of power or happiness or insight, especially if those paths have been marked off limits by the older generation.

Contacts with other cultures have brought into our lives information about the forces of evil. Voo-doo rites have been watched by our friends who have visited Haiti. Wycliffe translators share stories of their dealings with witch doctors who may live next door to them in an African or South American village. A couple of years ago the major news media carried reports of parties in San Jose, California, where people practicing white magic tried to brush demons out of the room with ostrich plumes. A tragic account from Switzerland captured our attention. It seems that a young girl was thought by her religious sect to be demon-possessed. To cure her, the members of the group beat her within an inch of her life, so frantically afraid were they of the evil powers.

Something else has contributed to this fear—our knowledge of the unspeakable atrocities that individuals and nations have committed in our lifetime. We have seen evil at work in ways that can be accounted for only on the basis of demon power. What else can rob whole civilizations of their sanity so they give themselves to ruthless aggression without regard for their own safety or other people's dignity? What else but Satan's power can lead a government to annihilate a whole race, as the citizens of that government stolidly and efficiently carry out their outrageous orders?

We have seen demon power snatching reason and decency from people who prided themselves on just those virtues. And who knows? Is our fear of evil powers sharpened by the gnawing suspicion that if the price were right we too might sell ourselves out? Is part of the terror that Satan holds over us our secret knowledge that we could become part of his team if he made the terms attractive enough? When we look in the mirror is it the likeness of Dr. Faust that we see, musing over that terrible transaction in which he sold himself to Satan?

Whatever the reason—fascination with the supernatural, interest in other cultures, awareness of the horrors of history, insight into the evils of our own spirits—whatever the reason, many of us live in fear of evil

73

powers. We need help to face this fear. And Jesus' lordship gives us this help.

JESUS CAN MASTER DEMONS

Jesus is admirably equipped to come to our rescue. Demons he knows all about; his life on earth was a series of encounters with evil or unclean spirits. The compassionate Savior went about doing good. Part of his healing ministry was to free people from the bondage of evil spirits that disturbed their reason and perverted their conduct. The Gospel writer Mark gives us a remarkable summary of this healing ministry: "Jesus withdrew with his disciples to the sea, and a great multitude from Galilee followed. . . . And he told his disciples to have a boat ready for him because of the crowd, lest they should crush him; for he had healed many, so that all who had diseases pressed upon him to touch him. And whenever the unclean spirits beheld him, they fell down before him and cried out, 'You are the Son of God.' "

Mark's language indicated that these were not isolated episodes but a regular pattern in Jesus' ministry. We should not see Jesus' struggles with demon powers as acts of kindness alone, the result of his deep concern for human suffering. Much more was involved.

Satan had dealt man a mortal blow at the beginning. His scheme successfully turned that first man and woman against God and against each other. His plot lured them out of the garden and into the wilderness. And as the centuries rolled by and man lived on the husks of his rebellion instead of the fruits of God's grace, Satan looked like a winner all the way.

Then Jesus came. Satan met him head on in the wilderness and tried to win the second and final fall. His triple testing failed; Jesus put him down. Final victory was in sight.

Wherever Jesus went he made it his business to deal decisively with the demons, those wicked spirits who took their orders from Satan. As he did, he was not only showing compassion for the wretched and the afflicted, he was demonstrating the power of his kingdom.

The devil's early victory over man brought great power to the kingdom of Satan. At times it seemed as though he ruled unopposed. What Christ was proving in conflict after conflict was that he, not Satan, was the real victor, the true Lord. And the demons recognized this. They confessed that Jesus was the Son of God more openly than the disciples had up to that point. In fact, Jesus had to hush them or they would have blurted out his true identity to the people before he was ready to reveal himself fully: "And he strictly ordered them not to make him known."

The evil spirits knew that their number was up. They knew that the end was near. The confusion and cruelty which had been their stock in trade could only be overcome by God's power. And this is just what they faced in Jesus—the power of God.

HISTORY MOVES TOWARD HIS COMING

Jesus' victory over Satan and his servants comes in stages. The second coming of Jesus toward which all history is moving is, of course, the final stage. Then Christ will bring down the curtain on all evil and reign as King of kings. Then it is that the terrible judgment will take place of which Jesus warned: "Depart from me, you cursed, into the eternal fire prepared for the devil and his angels" (Matt. 25:41).

Step by step he has been heading for that climax which is just as certain as his great acts in the past. His *death*, strange to say, was a crucial step in his victory over evil. One of Satan's greatest ploys is to make men think that they can reach God by keeping religious rules or practicing religious ceremonies. This cruel bit of deception Jesus exposed when he died for our sins and by his death built the only bridge by which man can cross to God. His death, then, was a victory over superstition and error.

The *resurrection* of Jesus was another stage in this victory. By defeating death, Jesus broke the main weapon that Satan and his followers used to terrorize the human family. Jesus defused the enemy's atom bomb when he went to the grave and came back again. That's why Jesus could claim that "All authority in heaven and on earth has been given unto me" (Matt. 28:18). Even the spirits that elude the grasp and sight of man and move elusively through the heavens are under Jesus' authority in the end. They can in no way block his program.

The other stage in Jesus' victory over the demons is his *ascension*, his triumphant return to the Father with the hero's welcome and the conqueror's laurels. This great homecoming is best described by Paul in Ephesians 1:20–22: God "raised him from the dead and made him sit at his right hand in the heavenly places, far above all rule and authority and power and dominion, . . . and he has put all things under his feet and has made him the head over all things for the church. . . ."

I don't think we need to push this further. We could add substantial comments on the fact that the ascended Christ poured out his Spirit on the church and that Spirit is the Spirit of power. We might take a second to remember that the ascended Christ prays for his own, and what evil spirit is a match for his prayers?

Trust Christ, that's all I'm saying. He is a winner, will be a winner at the end, has been all along. The right man is on our side, if we're on his. If God is for us, who can stand against us? Christ has beaten the devil's teams on every court where they have ever met. What we ought to do is stop fearing a possible defeat and start enjoying our actual victory.

Prayer: Father, sometimes when Satan churns the waters and our boats begin to bob, fear takes over. We don't want him to swamp our lives. At those stormy times, let the voice of your Son ring out above the waves: "Take heart, it is I; have no fear." In his powerful name we pray.

AMEN.

For further study of related themes refer to the following Scripture passages:

Acts 26:16–18
Ephesians 6:10–20
I John 2:14

Your Fear of Being Taken Advantage Of

IX

[38] "You have heard that it was said, 'An eye for an eye and a tooth for a tooth.' [39] But I say to you, Do not resist one who is evil. But if any one strikes you on the right cheek, turn to him the other also; [40] and if any one would sue you and take your coat, let him have your cloak as well; [41] and if any one forces you to go one mile, go with him two miles. [42] Give to him who begs from you, and do not refuse him who would borrow from you. . . ."

—MATTHEW 5:38–42

Hockey season is here. The newspapers, magazines, and TV news clips are full of pictures of swinging sticks, sailing pucks, and flashing skates. The goalie gets special attention. Crouched in his cage, coiled to block a shot, sprawled on the ice defending the goal with his body, he is the last line of defense. On his courage and quickness the game often turns.

You can always spot the goalie. He wears the most equipment—pads, gloves, mask. And he needs protection. Skaters that hurtle down the ice, sticks that slash like swords, pucks that fly like bullets pose constant threats to life and limb. The goalie does all that he can to defend himself in a game where danger is commonplace.

Many of us are just like a goalie. Next time you see a picture of a hockey goalie lurking behind his mask, shrouded in his pads, encased in his mitts, ask yourself how well defended you are against the hurts of life. In one way or another we seek to protect ourselves against uncertainty. One of our fears is that we will be taken advantage of.

Life seems to give us good reason for this fear. Old men abuse little girls for a few minutes of sick pleasure. Young men mug old women to buy one fix of heroin. We double lock our doors to prevent thievery. We double check our contracts to ward off trickery. We are afraid that people are going to take advantage of us.

Like the hockey goalie we pad ourselves with various kinds of insurance to protect us. In our large cities many women carry tear gas vials in their purses, while numbers of men carry guns in their cars. Both are forms of insurance against being taken advantage of. We carry literal insurance too, especially liability insurance against lawsuits which can wipe out all we have with one rap of the judge's gavel.

Even people who are trying to help someone in distress have to be careful. Sometimes doctors will not volunteer to help in emergencies because if things don't go right they can be sued. Many of us are leery of helping a stranded motorist along the highway or of picking up a hitchhiker. We have read too many stories of treachery or ambush in such situations.

So we go through life with eyes wary and guard up, watchful, suspicious, afraid. We pay a high price in time and energy to defend ourselves. We shut out strangers altogether and keep even friends at a distance, so that no one can take advantage of us.

We need help. We are afraid. A few words from Jesus make the difference. "You have heard that it was said, 'An eye for an eye and a tooth for a tooth.' But I say to you, Do not resist one who is evil."

These words are strong medicine, but they have to be to deal with the fears that have made us sick. Jesus is prescribing nothing less than a complete change of attitude toward those we fear will take advantage of us. Our defensiveness is so deep-seated that only a new and radical outlook on people can root it out.

Jesus gives examples in which we can discern three aspects our new outlook must have: first, an openness to be hurt rather than to hurt; second, a readiness to love people more than material goods; third, a willingness to do more for people than we need to do. In each case Jesus gives illustrations which are drawn from the culture of his day. Our task is to see the principle that lies behind the illustration.

An Openness to Be Hurt Rather Than to Hurt

The law of vengeance was built into the heart of clan life in Old Testament days. Any damage done to a member of your clan had to be avenged as soon as possible. The welfare and security of the clan were thought to be severely jeopardized until revenge could be taken.

Pride was fierce, and blood ran hot; no one could harm a strong man or his kin and get away with it.

In that kind of society the cycle of retaliation was unending. Blow called for blow; hurt demanded further hurt; wound could be healed only by another wound. Feuding became a way of life. When tribal and clan customs gave way to established law, vengeance was built into the process of law and was taken out of the hands of the clan. Punishment was inflicted, but only to the degree merited by the crime, and there the cycle was to stop: an eye for an eye, a tooth for a tooth. No more, no less. Exact vengeance.

But Jesus calls his people to live by a new pattern, not an endless feuding over who last hurt whom, not exact vengeance rendering cut for cut: "if any one strikes you on the right cheek, turn to him the other also." What Jesus demands is an openness to be hurt rather than to hurt. Forget about strict bookkeeping, Jesus says. Don't keep a careful ledger of the damage done to you by others. If you do, you will become bitter and hostile. Your retaliation may turn brutal and go far beyond anything the original hurt called for.

A slap on the cheek is not the signal for fifteen rounds of boxing. Absorb and ignore the slap. Chances are the person will not slap again. Let your trust in God control your temper. Your adversary's hostility is *his* problem basically, not *yours*. Don't add your fuel to his fire. Your calmness may help to bring him to his senses. It's worth a try.

HOW TO FACE YOUR FEARS

A Readiness to Love People More Than Material Goods

Jesus' second illustration touches our materialism as his first one speaks to our hostility. The illustration has to do with a lawsuit: "And if any one would sue you and take your coat, let him have your cloak as well." People may try to take advantage of us not only by physical harm but by legal damage as well.

If you're going to err, err on the side of generosity. That's Jesus' point. If someone thinks he is entitled to your inner tunic, give him your outer coat as well. Show him that material goods are not as important as he thinks they are.

My wife Ruth and I were chatting with a young woman on an airplane several months ago. She told us an incredible story of a conversation she had with a man who had broken into her apartment the night before. She found out he was hungry and lent him money. Beyond that she went so far as to offer him the use of her apartment for a weekend while she was away. I guess I looked shocked at the thought of her lending her apartment to a man who had planned to rob her. Seeing my look, she responded, "Well, what could I lose? Only my material possessions."

Learning to sit loose to our material possessions is part of Christian discipleship. If we are afraid that people are going to take advantage of us, we may need to develop a readiness to love people more than things. Jesus comes back to this at the close of our Scripture lesson: "Give to him who begs from you, and do not refuse him who would borrow from you." Contrast this advice with the words of old Polonius to his son Laertes in *Hamlet:* "Neither a borrower, nor a lender be; for loan oft loses both itself and friend, and borrowing dulls the edge of husbandry." Shrewd common sense is what the old man counseled. Loving concern is what Jesus advised. And there's a difference. Be of whatever financial help you can be to those who are in need. Let love control your pocketbook.

A WILLINGNESS TO DO MORE FOR PEOPLE THAN WE NEED TO DO

Jesus' third illustration comes from the realm of Roman law. A soldier or military official had a right to draft civilians to help carry his gear. These civilians, usually citizens of a country that the Roman army had invaded, were compelled to carry the soldier's burden a distance of one mile. Jesus asked of his disciples a readiness to do more for people than they need to: "And if any one forces you to go one mile, go with him two miles." Or, as Kenneth Taylor has translated this verse in *The Living Bible,* "If the military demand that you carry their gear for a mile, carry it two."

Think how this attitude can help liberate us from the fear of being taken advantage of. Where there is a readiness to do more than we need, we will rarely be bilked. Second-mile living puts the emphasis on what we can *do for* someone else, even an enemy as the Roman soldier was, not what he may *take from* us. A good offense is the best defense. We are less likely to be hurt when we cheerfully care for the needs of others than when we crouch in our defensive position, fearful that the world is going to run over us.

And if we do get hurt trying to do the right thing, we have the satisfaction of being in good company. Christ himself and his best followers lived this way and got great joy out of life. Love is hard to beat as a basic attitude.

For one thing, love is infectious. It absorbs hostility and encourages the other person to love in return. More than once enemies have been converted. Time and again people who thought to take advantage of us have been turned around by Christian love. Loving is what most people want to be. Aggressiveness, meanness, anger are often awkward cries for love. The perfect, mature love that casts out fear can sometimes satisfy that cry.

And even if it does not, we have high consolation. Love for our enemies, refusal to retaliate, generosity to their needs—all these link us to God's love. These attitudes line up our way of living with his: "Love your enemies and pray for those who persecute you, so that you may be sons of your Father who is in heaven; for he makes his sun rise on the evil and on the good, and sends rain on the just and on the unjust" (Matt. 5:44–45).

God's grace changed everything for us. He poured out his love into our lives when we were still sinners. He showed his goodness to us when we were dead set against him. And he calls us to live the same way.

Afraid of being taken advantage of? Learn to love. That's the answer. Shed your mask and pads, and open yourself to all that God has for you. You'll be surprised at how God will keep you from getting hurt. And you'll be pleased at how he'll stand by you and help you heal if you are hurt.

When the waves beat wild and the winds blow fierce, listen for the Savior's voice. He knows what it is to turn the other cheek and get slapped. He knows what it is to go the second mile, carrying a rugged cross. He knows what it is to give up not only his coat and cloak but his life in a crooked court of law. To us who are frozen by fear, he calls, "Take heart, it is I; have no fear." He knows what he's talking about. We'll do well to listen.

Prayer: Lord, we have so much to be fearful of. Well we know our inner weaknesses and our outer struggles. Help us to know your power and love even better. Show Jesus coming toward us, walking on the water. And by his voice erase our fears, for his sake. AMEN.

For further study of related themes refer to the following Scripture passages:

I Corinthians 6:7–8
I Thessalonians 5:15
I Peter 2:19–23

Your Fear
of Not Getting Credit
for Good Deeds

X

[1] "Beware of practicing your piety before men in order to be seen by them; for then you will have no reward from your Father who is in heaven.

[2] "Thus, when you give alms, sound no trumpet before you, as the hypocrites do in the synagogues and in the streets, that they may be praised by men. Truly, I say to you, they have their reward. [3] But when you give alms, do not let your left hand know what your right hand is doing, [4] so that your alms may be in secret; and your Father who sees in secret will reward you.

[5] "And when you pray, you must not be like the hypocrites; for they love to stand and pray in the synagogues and at the street corners, that they may be seen by men. Truly, I say to you, they have their reward. [6] But when you pray, go into your room and shut the door and pray to your Father who is in secret; and your Father who sees in secret will reward you. . . ."

—MATTHEW 6:1–6

It's the most boring part of a TV program, that dreary list of names at the end. The credits, they call it. Almost everybody who had anything to do with the show is mentioned: producer, associate producer, assistant producer; cameraman, sound man, makeup man; the man who arranges the lighting, the man who handles the props, the woman who designs the costumes; and, of course, all the actors and actresses. Line by line their names are given and their contribution to the show is stated.

Much of this the various unions and guilds require. But much of it is due to the audience's desire to know who played each part. We want to know whom to give credit to. For the same reason athletes wear numbers on their uniforms or jerseys. The team colors are not enough. We want to measure individual achievements: Who scored the touchdown? Who made the winning basket? Who leaped against the fence to catch the line drive?

I suppose it's natural and fitting for us to want to give credit where credit is due. A sterling performance in the concert hall deserves applause. A courageous effort on the playing field merits our cheers. But *giving* credit is one thing; *craving* credit is another. Being generous with our praise of others is noble; being desirous of praise for ourselves is vain.

Yet with many of us this desire is so strong it is virtually a fear—a fear of not getting credit for good deeds. We sit and watch the TV screens of life and long to see our names in the credits: credits for loyal service to the church, for kindness in the community, for generous support of Christian organizations. When the church bulletin publishes the list of those who served faithfully on the banquet committee, we are chagrined if our names are omitted.

At first glimpse, this fear of not getting credit for good deeds does not seem to be a serious problem. It's not a fear that sits like a brick in our stomach; it doesn't set our palms to sweating. Yet serious it really is. It can destroy our composure, unsettle our poise, rattle our relationships with others.

It is a dangerous fear, partly because we don't recognize it as such. We treat it as a normal kind of behavior. After all, doesn't everybody deserve credit for the good things he does? Isn't the approval we gain from others part of legitimate motivation in life? Praise is the spoonful of sugar that helps the medicine of hard work go down smoothly.

Jesus knew all about our drive for recognition and spoke to it directly: " 'Beware of practicing your piety before men in order to be seen by them; for then you will have no reward from your Father who is in heaven. . . . And when you pray, you must not be like the hypocrites; for they love to stand and pray in the synagogues and at the street corners, that they may be seen by men. Truly, I say to you, they have their reward.' "

These sharp words of Jesus show how subtle this problem is. Jesus is not warning us against open wickedness—murder, stealing, adultery. His subjects are acts of piety and the practice of prayer. He says that these can turn out badly if we are not careful. If you really want your deeds of charity and devotion to count, conquer your fear of not getting credit for them.

Your Fear of Not Getting Credit for Good Deeds

WHY WE HAVE FALSE FEARS

Though this is a false and foolish fear, it is a real one. It is false because it is misdirected; we should waste no energy wondering whether people have carefully noted how kind or how devout we are. It is real because we do waste energy on such wondering.

Why do we? Where does this false fear come from? To start with, it comes from *a low view of ourselves*. We look at the world around us and think that almost everyone else is taller and better than we are. It's hard to believe that we really count.

A lot of this, I suppose, stems from our childhood. We are anxious to please our parents and our teachers. One way we learn to please them is to do the right thing and then get credit for it.

A familiar story in the Hubbard family has to do with my brother Bob, now a pastor in the Panama Canal Zone. When he was a young tot, before I was born, he would wake up early on Christmas morning and run into our parents' bedroom. Then, with as cheery a voice as possible, he would call out, "Merry Christmas! Bobby." The good deed was there, a cordial Christmas greeting. But so was the desire for credit. It was not Paul, John, or Laura who wished the folks a merry Christmas; it was Bobby.

Each of us could tell similar stories from his own childhood. We sat in the front row of the classroom and tried to be called on first recitation time. We wanted the teacher's full approval. "Good for you, Charley," she would say, or, "That's exactly right, Sally." And we felt six inches taller.

A lot of this is normal, especially while we are learning our basic values and establishing our behavior patterns. Praise is one way of reinforcing our good deeds and encouraging wholesome habits.

Where we don't get a normal amount of encouragement, we can easily be conditioned to crave it. Starved for attention, we begin to wonder what's wrong with us. Then we begin to do extraordinary things to get attention. Sometimes the things are bad; the lying and stealing that young children do are often a cry for attention. Sometimes to gain this attention we begin a drive to excel in art or music or athletics. Almost without knowing it, we vow to show those tall people who paid us no attention that we do count. Our low view of ourselves pushes us to seek credit.

So does *our low view of God*. It is hard for us to believe that God would really pay attention to people as insignificant as we are. After all, if the earthly people around us, whose job it is to rear and train us, seem to neglect us, why would the Lord of heaven care?

What a mistake to make, to saddle God with the limitations and unkindnesses of our fallen humanity! Worrying too much about human credit for our acts of love and care may be a sure sign that we don't really trust God to do right by us.

What We Should Really Fear

Some may be tempted to react sharply to all this talk about not getting credit for good deeds. They may feel that it is not worth the effort to try at all. Doing good deeds and praying to God are hard enough as it is, without the added worry of whether we are doing them for the right reason. We may think, If I have to be that careful I won't bother to be either kind or devout. Purity of motive is so hard to come by that there is no use in my trying.

This kind of indifference is what we really should fear. Jesus did not leave good works or regular prayer as options: "when you give alms," Jesus said, and "when you pray." Not *if*. Do these things you must. It is how you do them that you must watch.

Alms-giving and prayer are symbols of our two highest duties, love for neighbor and love for God. They are essential human acts. Without them we cannot really live a human life. Kindness to men and communion with God—these are the twin centers around which life pivots. No one can pull away from either of these without leaving part of his humanity behind.

What we really should fear, then, is disobedience to God's two great commandments. Failure to love— that's what we should be afraid of. And Jesus' words, though they seem harsh, are designed to guard us against this dreaded failure to love which makes us less than men.

Jesus warns us not to worry about getting human credit for what we do. If credit is foremost on our minds, our good works are not really good because they are done for our own benefit. If attention is foremost on our minds, our prayers are not really prayers because they are a show to impress others, not sincere worship of God.

We become hypocrites—actors, show-offs, pretenders

—and Jesus' words for them are biting: "Thus, when you give alms, sound no trumpet before you, as the hypocrites do in the synagogues and in the streets, that they may be praised by men. Truly, I say to you, they have their reward." And again, "And when you pray, you must not be like the hypocrites; for they love to stand and pray in the synagogues and at the street corners, that they may be seen by men. Truly, I say to you, they have their reward."

Jesus' remedy for this kind of hypocrisy is a strong one: Lean over as far backward as possible from the temptation to put on a public show as you perform your acts of kindness to men and devotion to God. Put down by drastic means your fear of not getting credit. "But when you give alms, do not let your left hand know what your right hand is doing, so that your alms may be in secret; and your Father who sees in secret will reward you." And similarly, "But when you pray, go into your room and shut the door and pray to your Father who is in secret; and your Father who sees in secret will reward you."

Good deeds rendered so quietly that *you* hardly know what you've done, let alone anyone else; a life of prayer so removed from the eye of others as to remain a secret between you and your Father—this is Christ's remedy for our hypocritical tendencies. Deeds done this quietly and devotion rendered this privately have the best chance of remaining true acts of love and worship.

Do what is right, and leave the results to God. When you do, the love will be truer and the rewards greater. Forget about rewards, and divine rewards will come.

Have your mind on rewards, and human rewards are the best you can hope for. And they are not worth much.

These words of Jesus can set us free, if we'll let them—free from the worry of watching the TV screens and bulletin boards of life to see our names appear, free from the concern over whether others think we are spiritual or not. Leave the credits to the actors and the athletes. Disciples don't need them. The gracious deeds and the devout moments carry their own satisfaction. They are what the Master requires, and he knows what is best for us.

This fear of not getting credit may not seem as threatening as some that we face. But it will sink us if we let it. Here as in the other storms, the best words come from Jesus: "Take heart, it is I; have no fear." Trust God, and get on with what you are called to do. You'll enjoy life a whole lot more if you don't look around to see who's watching. Look out for the needs of others, and look up to your Father who knows all about you. In those two looks lies the meaning of life. Don't miss it by looking in the wrong direction.

Prayer: Heavenly Father, thank you for helping us over this hump, this hump of being so desperately concerned about what people think of our righteousness. Help us to see that it is Christ's righteousness which really counts, and no one can call that into question. We want to worship you and serve others. Teach us so to lose ourselves in those grand enterprises that we won't trifle with trivial issues like human credit. In Christ's all-knowing name, we pray.
AMEN.

For further study of related themes refer to the following Scripture passages:

Matthew 5:20
Matthew 6:19–21
Acts 5:1–6

Your Fear of Being Misled Spiritually

¹⁵ "Beware of false prophets, who come to you in sheep's clothing but inwardly are ravenous wolves. ¹⁶ You will know them by their fruits. Are grapes gathered from thorns, or figs from thistles? ¹⁷ So, every sound tree bears good fruit, but the bad tree bears evil fruit. ¹⁸ A sound tree cannot bear evil fruit, nor can a bad tree bear good fruit. ¹⁹ Every tree that does not bear good fruit is cut down and thrown into the fire. ²⁰ Thus you will know them by their fruits.

²¹ "Not every one who says to me, 'Lord, Lord,' shall enter the kingdom of heaven, but he who does the will of my Father who is in heaven. ²² On that day many will say to me, 'Lord, Lord, did we not prophesy in your name, and cast out demons in your name, and do many mighty works in your name?' ²³ And then will I declare to them, 'I never knew you; depart from me, you evildoers. . . .' "

—MATTHEW 7:15–23

We have received some disturbing letters lately, letters sent both to "The Joyful Sound" broadcast and to Fuller Theological Seminary. A typical one might read like this:

For years my husband and I have been faithful members of our church. My husband has served on the

95

board, and I have taught a Sunday school class. A few months ago my husband began to take an interest in another religious group, a *sect*, I would call it. Now all he reads is their literature; he listens to their broadcasts; he argues for their beliefs. I don't know what to do. Our children are being confused; our marriage is being torn apart.

These letters are symptoms of one of the sharp fears of our times, the fear of being misled spiritually. Our civilization is especially vulnerable to this fear, because it offers us so many religious choices. In most cultures, particularly in times past, the people of a given tribe or nation had one religion. Everybody believed it; everybody practiced it. It was an essential part of their way of life, taken for granted by almost all the people.

In our day and in our western world—Europe and the Americas—the situation is different. Most European countries were almost uniformly Catholic until the Protestant Reformation. Then the picture became more complex. Some countries like Spain and Portugal remained Catholic. Others, like Norway and Sweden, became almost entirely Protestant. Others, like Germany, were divided, part Protestant and part Catholic. Protestantism itself took many shapes—Anglican under Henry VIII in England; Calvinist in Switzerland, Holland, Scotland, and parts of France; Lutheran in Germany and Scandinavia; and Anabaptist in several countries, particularly Holland, Germany, and England.

All of these European church traditions were brought to the New World after the pilgrims landed. Here further division and multiplication took place as the nation moved its frontiers farther and farther west. During this process some leaders claimed to gain fresh light from the Scriptures and founded new groups. Others felt they had special revelation in the form of visions or new sacred writings, and they gathered eager followers around them.

The results of this religious diversification are obvious. Look at the church page of Saturday's newspaper in any large city. It offers more varieties of religion than a well-stocked cafeteria does of food. No wonder we are afraid of being misled spiritually. There are so many options to choose from, each offering its answers to our problem in what seems to be a sincere and attractive way.

The people who feel most keenly this fear of making the wrong choice are often the best people. They care. They want to do the right thing. They don't take their decisions casually. They believe that spiritual things are of utmost importance.

Among these sensitive people today are numbers of our young people, people of high school or college age, who are seeking spiritual values and spiritual experience in increasing numbers. Many of them have already been burned by bad choices. Rebellion, violence, drugs, rejection of parents, sexual freedom—these have left their scars. Tenderly, gingerly, these young people test the spiritual claims of those who call for their allegiance.

And they should. This is just what Jesus taught his followers to do. In stern terms he alerted them to the dangers inherent in spiritual decision, especially the danger of following the wrong leader: "Beware of false prophets, who come to you in sheep's clothing but inwardly are ravenous wolves."

THE TEMPTATIONS OF FALSE LEADERSHIP

Leadership is heady wine. There can be an almost intoxicating exhilaration in getting people to follow you. They trust your judgment, seek your counsel, argue for your cause, tend to your needs, and build your self-esteem.

People are tempted to become leaders of religious groups because of their *arrogance*. They feel they have something fresh to say, something new to bring. The church has had it wrong up till now or has missed part of the truth. And these leaders generously volunteer to set things straight.

Often they pretend to be loyal to the Scriptures. They quote verses freely and pay tribute to God's Word generously. But when you check closely you find that they neglect some parts of Scripture and over-emphasize others. Or you may find that they honor Scripture but actually take their authority from other books or from their own private insights. In either case their arrogant confidence in their own beliefs, together with suspicion of other people's views, has prompted them to assume leadership.

Ambition as well as arrogance may tempt them to snatch the reins and drive off in some wild direction to gain a following. Leadership can carry with it a great sense of power. Egos can be fed; fortunes can be accumulated; lasting monuments can be erected. All one needs is a substantial following.

"Ravenous wolves" are what Jesus calls these false prophets. They don't feed the flock; they feed *on* them. Pretending to be part of God's people, they move among the sheep with destructive results.

Honest people have been bilked out of their life savings. Sincere people have been separated from their families. Hard-working people have quit their jobs. Devout people have been seduced into heresy. Moral people have been taught to violate their consciences. And all this in the name of some smooth, suave, so-called prophet who built his own prestige at terrible cost to God's people.

But the fault does not lie with the impostor alone, this wolf in sheep's clothing. The sheep often contribute to the temptation that false leaders face.

They have their own problems of *pride*. It's exciting to belong to an in group, a private truth club. We feel informed, full of new ideas. We feel finely righteous, uniquely set apart by God. Knowing more and believing better than other groups in the church, we can develop a sense of smugness that makes us feel proud of ourselves and sorry for everyone else.

Gullibility as well as pride is a problem of the followers. It is almost as though we want to be deceived. Our naïveté contributes to the temptation that false leaders give in to. Refusing to think for ourselves, we turn over all spiritual responsibility to them. Their arrogance we confuse with wisdom. Because they seem to know their own minds, we cease to use our own.

The Tests of True Leadership

This is just what Jesus is trying to keep us from doing. His command is: Put the lives and claims of these would-be leaders to the test. "You will know them by their fruits. Are grapes gathered from thorns, or figs from thistles? So, every sound tree bears good fruit, but the bad tree bears evil fruit. A sound tree cannot bear evil fruit, nor can a bad tree bear good fruit. Every tree that does not bear good fruit is cut down and thrown into the fire. Thus you will know them by their fruits."

Leadership, true or false, is to be tested by its fruit. This is tricky, because Jesus has already warned us about the dangers of judging: "Judge not, that you be not judged. For with the judgment you pronounce you will be judged, and the measure you give will be the measure you get" (Matt. 7:1–2). Don't try to read people's motives or hearts. And don't criticize them harshly for faults that you have as well. This seems to be the gist of Jesus' warning.

But where religious teachers are involved, tests must be applied. Their fruit must be carefully inspected. We might be baffled by what Jesus means by fruit if he had not expanded some on his comments in the next verses.

Profession of faith is not the real test, Jesus warns: "Not every one who says to me, 'Lord, Lord,' shall enter the kingdom of heaven." This does not mean that we should doubt everybody's profession and refuse to accept them as Christian leaders until we can put them to a prolonged test. It does mean that profession is not enough. There are those who claim to be Christ's men whom he in turn will not claim.

I don't think we should let our fear of being spiritually misled make us neurotic, but it should make us cautious. We can accept a person's claim to be a spokesman for Christ at face value. We can receive him in good faith and then hear what he has to say. All the time we have to bear in mind the possibility that he may say, "Lord, Lord," and not really belong to Christ.

Spiritual achievement is not the real test any more than profession of faith is. This is a helpful warning because all of us are impressed by deeds of spiritual power. "On that day many will say to me, 'Lord, Lord, did we not prophesy in your name, and cast out demons in your name, and do many mighty works in your name?' And then will I declare to them, 'I never knew you; depart from me, you evildoers.' "

I'm glad we have Christ's authority on this subject, because it would be difficult for us to come to this conclusion on our own. It seems so harsh.

But spiritual achievement is both hard to detect and difficult to measure. God's Spirit is not the only spirit at work in the world. Human spirits can perform startling accomplishments in mass manipulation, in psychic exhilaration, in crowd hysteria. The excitement of the moment can spur people to super-human achievements. Demon power may also be at work in the world. Like Pharaoh's magicians in the days of Moses, they may duplicate or counterfeit some of the works of God.

Not profession of faith, not spiritual achievement, but *obedience to the will of God is the real test* of true spiritual leadership: "Not every one who says to me, 'Lord, Lord,' shall enter the kingdom of heaven, but he who does the will of my Father who is in heaven."

"He who does the will of my Father"—this is the person to follow. Mind you, Jesus does not say, He who *claims* to know the will of my Father. Not secret information but basic obedience is what Jesus stresses.

How do we know whether a professed spiritual leader is doing the will of God? We test his words and life by the Word of God. The will of God is not a matter of hunch or intuition, not a matter of private knowledge or personal revelation. Nothing can be within the will of God which clashes with the teaching of the Word of God.

A person who defies God's Word by living an immoral or unrighteous life is not doing the will of God. An individual who violates Christ's commandments by being unjust, harsh, or greedy is not doing the will of God.

Especially crucial to the ministry of any person or group is what it teaches about Jesus Christ. Is he regularly proclaimed as God's eternal Son who took on human nature to die for our sins and to rise again bodily? Is he coming again in power and glory to save his people and judge the world? No teacher or congregation can truly do God's will without being fully loyal to what the Bible teaches us about Jesus.

Some closing words of advice may be in order. First, don't be hasty in making judgments about spiritual leadership. It may take a little time for you to decide whether or not the leadership is teaching and doing

God's will. Second, don't be faddish about taking up new ideas. In the long history of Christ's church, most new ideas in doctrine have proved wrong. The odds are slim that what is new is actually true. Third, go with Christ. Find your fellowship where his name is honored, where his power is trusted, where his message is cherished, where his teachings are practiced. Anything that detracts from his glory should be automatically suspect.

He it was who appeared in the dark of the night to perplexed disciples and calmed their fears: "Take heart, it is I; have no fear." His words, his love, his forgiveness are still our best weapons against all fear, especially the fear of being spiritually misled.

Prayer: Heavenly Father, thank you for showing us your truth in a person. Him we can understand. His teaching, his life, his saving works show us the difference between good fruit and bad. Make him, Father, so large in our lives that false teaching has no chance. In his righteous name we pray.

AMEN.

For further study of related themes refer to the following Scripture passages:

I Timothy 4:1–3
II Peter 2:1–4
I John 4:1–3

Your Fear XII
of Costly Discipleship

²⁵ At that time Jesus declared, "I thank thee, Father, Lord of heaven and earth, that thou hast hidden these things from the wise and understanding and revealed them to babes; ²⁶ yea, Father, for such was thy gracious will. ²⁷ All things have been delivered to me by my Father; and no one knows the Son except the Father, and no one knows the Father except the Son and any one to whom the Son chooses to reveal him. ²⁸ Come to me, all who labor and are heavy laden, and I will give you rest. ²⁹ Take my yoke upon you, and learn from me; for I am gentle and lowly in heart, and you will find rest for your souls. ³⁰ For my yoke is easy, and my burden is light."
—MATTHEW 11:25–30

Why doesn't everyone who hears the message of God's love for the world through Jesus become a Christian? Have you ever asked yourself that question? I suppose that it can be answered from a number of angles.

Some don't respond because they don't believe that the great events of Jesus' birth, life, death, and resurrection really happened. They have not examined the thorough Gospel accounts; they have not checked the vast amount of historical evidence that confirms these accounts. The mystery of how God could become man is too much for them to credit, so they disregard the Christian faith as something that asks them to believe more than they are prepared to.

People like this we should patiently and lovingly challenge to examine the facts, to dig into the Gospel stories, to open themselves to the words of Jesus. God's Spirit, which has encouraged scores of millions of believers through the centuries, may yet work his grace in their hearts and lead them to faith in the divine Son of God.

Others don't respond because they see nothing unusual or exciting about the way Christians live. They are like the Indian philosopher who saw in Christians "a lot of ordinary people making extraordinary claims." Satisfied with their own lives, these unbelievers don't see enough difference in the lives of Christians around them to prompt them to change.

People like these we have a special responsibility to. Their unbelief may not be our fault, but we have given them few good reasons to cast their lot with Christ. The quality of our love, the exuberance of our joy, the clarity of our beliefs need looking to. If we have acted as though God's good news of love for the world is another ho-hum message, shame on us. We need to hear it again and recover its excitement.

Still others don't respond to the Christian message because of what they think are its terrifying demands. They are afraid, afraid of costly discipleship. When you think about it, the implications of this fear are horrendous. The good news of the Gospel is altered so drastically that it becomes a story of human bondage, not of human liberation. The theme is no longer God's love but God's demands. The major emphasis is no longer grace but duty.

Whatever keeps men and women from serving Christ is a tragedy. But the worst tragedy of all is to turn your back on the Savior because you think the price of his friendship is too high.

Jesus has words for all our fears, but to none does he speak more directly than to this one. He asked for allegiance, all right, but he tried to put this allegiance in terms that we could respond to. As the master teacher he was recruiting students, students who would be influenced by his life and would spread his beliefs. Now, students who are going to work closely with a master want to know two things above all about that teacher: How much does he know? How does he treat his students?

Years ago, when I was completing my doctoral studies at St. Andrews University in Scotland, I went to see my professor. I could tell that he was in a serious mood when he said, "Now before we talk, please sit down and read this letter I have written to you." It was a long letter on legal-size paper, typed on both sides. In it he had evaluated my work, thoroughly and somewhat critically. The upshot of our conversation was that I was to add another substantial chapter to the book I was writing and thoroughly revise several others. This revision meant that I had to stay a couple of months longer in Scotland than I had planned, and I had already been separated from my wife and daughter for four months.

The professor seemed almost apologetic for being so critical. I tried to put him at ease. "The reason that I came here was to take advantage of your wisdom and knowledge in this subject. The books on my topic I could have read in the U.S.A., but I wanted your supervision, your wisdom, your time." And I had gotten them, though on that particular day they had proved a bit disheartening.

What we want in a good teacher, Jesus has in full measure: knowledge and concern. As we see who he is we can learn to handle our fear, our fear of costly discipleship.

Jesus' Credentials As a Teacher

How much does Jesus know? This is our first question as we ask whether we can wholly commit our lives to him. If he is to be our tutor in things eternal, we must have a look at his credentials.

One way to do this is to overhear one of his most moving prayers, uttered in a moment of sublime intimacy that he enjoyed with his Father: "At that time Jesus declared, 'I thank thee, Father, Lord of heaven and earth, that thou hast hidden these things from the wise and understanding and revealed them to babes; yea, Father, for such was thy gracious will. All things have been delivered to me by my Father; and no one knows the Son except the Father, and no one knows the Father except the Son and any one to whom the Son chooses to reveal him.' "

How are these for credentials? Full authority of the Father delivered into his hand, exclusive knowledge of the Father reserved for him and anyone he lets in on it.

Are you looking for a spiritual tutor, someone to guide you into the truth of God? Look no further. There is no way to improve on Jesus Christ. All the vagueness of man's quest for God can be set aside. Precise, full, intimate knowledge of the Father is available. Jesus has an exclusive claim to it, but he offers to share it with those who love and trust him.

Talk about great teachers, the number-one question of the universe he can answer. What is God like? That's the sixty-four-dollar question, sixty-four-million-dollar—forget the price; it's worth everything. That's *the* question of the human spirit. Philosophers have mused upon it; artists have tried to catch it on canvas; musicians have searched for lost chords to capture it; poets have written volumes to express it. Jesus alone has answered it.

On the subject of God, he is the only teacher worth having. Everyone else guesses; he knows. Compared with him, the religious experts of the world are still in kindergarten. For his kind of knowledge, our discipleship with him is worth any cost.

Jesus' Treatment of His Students

Sometimes the teachers who know the most are hardest to get along with. Their intelligence is so keen and their knowledge so encyclopedic that they lack patience with their students. A friend of mine, a distinguished eye doctor, once worked with a world-famous surgeon. The surgeon on a given day would ask a highly technical question in a casual, offhand manner. Because my friend wanted to learn as much as he could, he would work half the night to dig out the answer. When the surgeon brought up the question the next day, my friend was ready. But less diligent students were ruthlessly clobbered for their dullness or indifference. The surgeon's high-strung brilliance made life difficult for everyone around him.

Not so with Jesus. He did not use his amazing knowledge of God to put down his students. He was a teacher, not a show-off. Because knowledge of God is healing, peace-bringing, joy-giving knowledge, it has an uplifting, restful character to it.

It is this that Jesus offers in his famous invitation where he reveals how he intends to treat his students: "Come to me, all who labor and are heavy laden, and I will give you rest. Take my yoke upon you, and learn from me; for I am gentle and lowly in heart, and you will find rest for your souls. For my yoke is easy, and my burden is light."

This is an invitation *staggering in its scope*. Compare it with most of the invitations that we send out. They are limited to a few friends who will attend a party; they are issued only to the members of the club called to a special meeting; they are sold only to those who can pay the price of admission to the ball game or concert; they are extended to the chosen few who will fill the number of employment opportunities still open at the office.

But with Jesus the situation is different. His invitation is open to all comers: "Come to me, all who labor and are heavy laden." That takes in all of us, doesn't it? Burdened with our work, feeling the pressure of caring for our families, fighting the stress and strain that come with modern life, we surely qualify among those whom Jesus calls.

And this is an invitation *encouraging in its promise:* "I will give you rest." Most of the invitations we receive ask something of us. The boss invites us to spend our time and energy in ways that help the company; the family reminds us of our responsibilities to support and sustain it; the club sends us a bill for our dues. Jesus says, "I will give you rest." Can anyone really turn him down?

One more thing, this is an invitation *gentle in its demands.* The promise of rest precedes the offer of the yoke. Responsibility there will be. That's what the yoke means: "Take my yoke upon you, and learn from me. ... For my yoke is easy, and my burden is light."

Christian discipleship is not a party or picnic. But before the work begins, the beautiful rest is afforded. Rested from the burden of our empty lives, we have the energy to shoulder Christ's yoke. As the ox was yoked to pull the cart or draw the sled or thresh the grain, so we are yoked to carry out the Master's mission.

The yoke is carefully fitted, as Jesus the carpenter undoubtedly tried to do in his days at Nazareth. Hand-worked to suit our shoulders, it does not bind or chafe: "my yoke is easy" is his promise. And the work he calls us to do is within our capabilities. Ours is neither a high-handed nor hardhearted Master. He himself became a servant for us, so he knows what our lot is like. "Gentle and lowly in heart" is the way he describes himself.

Teach he does, and *learn* we must. That's what being Master and disciple involves. But his lessons are within our abilities, and his demands are in keeping with the gifts he has given. He knows his subject and cares for his students, an ideal combination.

So we can have another look at this fear of ours, this fear of costly discipleship. Jesus is ready to deal with it, as ready as he was during that fearful night when his disciples clung to the sides of a bouncing boat, drenched with terror, until they heard his voice: "Take heart, it is I; have no fear." That same voice calls, Come to me. Put away your fears. Learn from me. Work with me. Let me give you rest.

Costly discipleship? In a way, yes. It will cost us our stubborn rebellion, our burning guilt, our foolish aimlessness. But it will give us what we most need and least find: true knowledge of the Father whom the Son knows to perfection; true rest from all that burdens our hearts and wearies our spirits; true work in history's greatest endeavor with the universe's finest Master. On these terms, what is really costly is not to come.

Prayer: Heavenly Father, once again you have helped us get perspective on our fears. As usual we see that they were not worth fearing. Teach us to fear you and learn where true wisdom begins. Learners—that's what we long to be, now that we see Jesus as the master teacher and your love as his subject. Thank you for inviting us to study with him. In his name we pray.

AMEN.

For further study of related themes refer to the following Scripture passages:

Mark 14:50–52
Luke 18:18–30
John 18:25–27

Your Fear XIII
of Breaking
with Tradition

¹ On a sabbath, while he was going through the grainfields, his disciples plucked and ate some ears of grain, rubbing them in their hands. ² But some of the Pharisees said, "Why are you doing what is not lawful to do on the sabbath?" ³ And Jesus answered, "Have you not read what David did when he was hungry, he and those who were with him: ⁴ how he entered the house of God, and took and ate the bread of the Presence, which it is not lawful for any but the priests to eat, and also gave it to those with him?" ⁵ And he said to them, "The Son of man is lord of the sabbath."

⁶ On another sabbath, when he entered the synagogue and taught, a man was there whose right hand was withered. ⁷ And the scribes and the Pharisees watched him, to see whether he would heal on the sabbath, so that they might find an accusation against him. ⁸ But he knew their thoughts, and he said to the man who had the withered hand, "Come and stand here." And he rose and stood there. ⁹ And Jesus said to them, "I ask you, is it lawful on the sabbath to do good or to do harm, to save life or to destroy it?" ¹⁰ And he looked around on them all, and said to him, "Stretch out your hand." And he did so, and his hand was restored. ¹¹ But they were filled with fury and discussed with one another what they might do to Jesus.

—LUKE 6:1–11

The people at the party suddenly grew tense. The discussion had been congenial and at times exciting. We had been talking about the way God was working in the world, the signs of spiritual renewal, the breakthroughs in mission overseas. Then we began to talk about the Jesus people. And that's when things grew tense.

"I doubt the sincerity of these kids," confessed one of my friends. "Their manner seems so casual and their taste so questionable. Worse still, they speak of God in such irreverent, intimate terms that they make me squirm."

"That's right," chimed in one of the lovely women. "They seem to ignore the majesty, the holiness of God."

"Now wait a minute," interrupted a businessman who had spent years working with college students. "I know a lot of these kids, and I've been impressed by their devotion to the Savior. Their language, dress, and music may not suit our tastes, but we should respect their Christian commitment and encourage them in it. Their way of expressing their faith may prove a lot more attractive to our young people than ours has. Besides, we have to remember that some of these kids whose style upsets us belong to us."

At about that point the topic took a turn without either side changing its mind. In those few minutes the people at the party were brought face to face with one of the most constant and urgent questions that we Christians face: How do we view the changes taking place as the generations come and go? Or to put it another way: Should we fear the sharp breaks with tradition that we see all around us? My friend who first broached the subject at the party was obviously afraid, and so were several others who shared his point of view. Weeks later I was back in that city and found that the discussion was still going on.

It was fear of breaking with tradition that made Jewish leaders, like the Pharisees, suspicious of Jesus. They felt it their solemn duty to protect the tradition because the tradition protected the law. "Fencing the Torah" is what the Jews called this. They were so fearful of breaking the Old Testament law that they built another set of laws like a wall around it. For instance, the Old Testament contains this command: "You shall not boil a kid in its mother's milk" (Exod. 23:19). God's people were warned against this because it was a Canaanite magical practice. Israel's pagan neighbors thought that they could lay hold of special spiritual power by cooking a young goat in its mother's milk. But this kind of magic was to have no place in the lives of God's chosen people. They were to trust God, not magic, for power and protection.

Around this commandment Jewish tradition built a fence. It taught that no milk and meat should be eaten together, in order to make sure that the commandment was not violated. After all, how can one be dead sure that he is not mixing a kid with his mother's milk unless he makes it a point never to eat milk or cheese with meat?

This kind of attachment to tradition is an example of a devotion to the letter of the law that misses the spirit of it completely. Jesus came to fulfill the law but not to defend the tradition. Two episodes recorded in Luke's Gospel make this clear.

One day Jesus and his disciples were strolling through a grainfield. Almost instinctively the disciples reached for a few ears of grain and plucked them. Then they rubbed the grain in their hands to loosen the husk. Probably they blew on the grain lightly to drive away the chaff with a puff of breath. Then they ate the kernels. An innocent act, something that every farm boy has done when he wanted a snack.

Yet the Pharisees, as self-appointed guardians of tradition, were outraged. Why? The grain plucking was done on the sabbath. According to the Pharisees, Jesus' men had violated their interpretation of the sabbath command: "Remember the sabbath day, to keep it holy. Six days you shall labor, and do all your work; but the seventh day is a sabbath to the Lord your God; in it you shall not do any work, you, or your son, or your daughter, your manservant, or your maidservant, or your cattle, or the sojourner who is within your gates" (Exod. 20:8–10).

Around this commandment Jewish tradition had built a fence by carefully defining what was work and what was not. The disciples had not violated the spirit of the command. They were not laboring in the fields with sickle and scythe. They had not tied their flowing tunics tight around their loins and girded themselves for hard work. No oxen had been yoked to help them haul and thresh the grain. On a sabbath stroll, they merely plucked a few ears and enjoyed a morsel or two. Yet their accusers called this work and acted as though heaven and earth would collapse. They were afraid to break with tradition themselves and viewed with suspicion and anger anyone who did.

The second episode is even more shocking. It shows how deeply fearful of change the Pharisees were, how dearly they treasured their traditions. Jesus, as usual, had gone to the synagogue on the sabbath. The Pharisees and scribes, who gave instruction in the Jewish laws, were there too. And so was a man with a shriveled hand. All eyes were on him. Would Jesus again violate the sabbath by healing him? He knew their thoughts and deliberately defied their authority by openly healing the man with the deformed hand.

"Filled with fury" is how Luke describes the reaction of the Jewish leaders. Think how their fear distorted their perspective. One of their neighbors had been healed. Gone was the handicap that hampered his attempts to earn a living. Gone was the stigma that caused adults to look away and little children to stare. He had been healed, made whole, ready to join society as an accepted, responsible member. This was a day for high rejoicing, but not for the Pharisees and scribes. In their book healing was work: "they were filled with fury and discussed with one another what they might do to Jesus."

They had just watched a healing, yet they had murder on their minds. Their attachment to tradition was stronger than their appreciation of Jesus' miracle. This is a blind attachment based on fear. And we could be harsh with these Jewish teachers, if we did not suffer from some of the same fears ourselves. What miracles are we missing because we are so tightly tied to our past?

One clear lesson that we learn from these sabbath-day episodes is that we must test tradition. Tradition is not automatically bad, and change is not necessarily good. We have to weigh each issue individually, and these two stories give us help as we do. The first story teaches us to test tradition by the lordship of Jesus; the second story teaches us to test tradition by the law of love—the lordship of Jesus and the law of love.

TESTING TRADITION BY THE LORDSHIP OF JESUS

"Why are you doing what is not lawful to do on the sabbath?" the Pharisees asked Jesus and his men after they had plucked a few grains and eaten them. Jesus' answer was full of power and courage. He reminded them of a time when King David, one of the Pharisees' heroes, in an emergency entered the Tabernacle with his men and ate some of the bread that was supposedly restricted for the priests (I Sam. 21:6). The revered king of Israel exercised his authority in a time of need and was not condemned for it. How much more, Jesus argues, do I have a right to exercise my authority on the sabbath? The priests recognized the king's right, and the Pharisees should recognize the rights of the King of kings. "The Son of man is lord of the sabbath" was the blunt way Jesus put it.

What's at stake in the matter of tradition is nothing less than Jesus' right as Lord of the universe to bring change, to do things another way. How do we test tradition by Jesus' lordship? We do just what Jesus did. We use the Scriptures as the rule by which to check traditions.

Styles of dress, grooming, and music, forms of teaching, worship, or organization in the church are often the result of custom. For some people they take on a fixedness as though they were God-ordained, revealed in his Word. Change any part of the way they do things and they are at sea, adrift, wondering where to go, what to do. Their composure is ruffled; their security is unhinged. They may be anxious or even angry.

But we need not react this way. The Bible can lead us beyond anxiety and anger. It gives us the grounds by which we judge which traditions should be cherished and which should be discarded. Whatever we hold that does not square with Scripture we should hold lightly. If need be, we should give it up. Let Jesus be Lord of all traditions and, by his Word, lead us to decide what needs changing and what does not.

TESTING TRADITION BY THE LAW OF LOVE

"I ask you," said Jesus to the Pharisees who did not want him to heal on the sabbath because they considered healing as work, "is it lawful on the sabbath to do good or to do harm, to save life or to destroy it?" His question drove to the heart of their problem. Keeping the law was more important to them than doing good. Worse still, in the name of good they were doing evil. Trying to be righteous, they became loveless.

The need for good works, the need to save life, surely takes priority over custom, Jesus observes. What kind of righteousness would it be to cling to tradition, while people all around are being hurt by it? Where tradition wars against love for people, tradition should be scrapped. Traditions ought to serve and help people, not the other way around. Test tradition by the law of love. That's what Jesus did. His love moved him to heal, whether the tradition and its defenders liked it or not.

In spite of all I've said, a word to tradition-breakers may be in order. *If some people cling too tightly to traditions, don't think you have to smash them too sharply.* Christians may have to challenge harmful traditions just as Jesus did. But challenging traditions does not make one a Christian. Jesus may have had some revolutionary traits, but this does not mean that he approves of all revolutions or revolutionaries. Christ's lordship as expressed in the Scripture and his love as demonstrated in the Gospels ought to govern what we do and how we do it. Trigger-happy rebels, ready to take pot shots at most of what goes on in the church, need to learn this.

But a word to tradition-guarders is also in order. *Make sure that what you cherish is worth it.* Noble traditions can become outworn relics. Patterns that once held life and meaning for God's people can become dead forms. Christ's lordship and love must have the final say. Don't let your love for the status quo rob you of the joy of seeing things change for the better. God is on the move in the world today. Why don't you go with him?

A lot of church parties have been made tense in recent years as good people have talked about puzzling changes. The one I sat in on will come out all right because the people there are willing to let Jesus be Lord. He will be anyway, you know. The real question is not his lordship but our obedience. About that we can do something.

Prayer: Lord, give us the steadfastness to hold to what can never be changed—your love, your power, your purposes. And give us, too, the flexibility to change whatever is not worth hanging onto. Above all, give us the wisdom through your Word to make the distinction between changeless truth and changing tradition. Free us from fighting feverish battles over foolish causes. Let Christ's love and Christ's lordship guide us in all we do.

AMEN.

For further study of related themes refer to the following Scripture passages:

Matthew 12:9–14
Mark 7:1–13
Colossians 2:20–23

¹⁷ Now when Jesus came, he found that Lazarus had already been in the tomb four days. ¹⁸ Bethany was near Jerusalem, about two miles off, ¹⁹ and many of the Jews had come to Martha and Mary to console them concerning their brother. ²⁰ When Martha heard that Jesus was coming, she went and met him, while Mary sat in the house. ²¹ Martha said to Jesus, "Lord, if you had been here, my brother would not have died. ²² And even now I know that whatever you ask from God, God will give you." ²³ Jesus said to her, "Your brother will rise again." ²⁴ Martha said to him, "I know that he will rise again in the resurrection at the last day." ²⁵ Jesus said to her, "I am the resurrection and the life; he who believes in me, though he die, yet shall he live, ²⁶ and whoever lives and believes in me shall never die. Do you believe this?" ²⁷ She said to him, "Yes, Lord; I believe that you are the Christ, the Son of God, he who is coming into the world."

—JOHN 11:17–27

My young friend suddenly tightened as we walked into the dark together. "I'm getting bad vibrations," he said and pointed to an old hearse on the parking lot. It had been years since that hearse had performed its appointed duty for a local funeral home. Now it carried students and surfboards, groceries and baby buggies. Yet the old association was there, and my friend felt it.

Perhaps he felt it more intensely because we had been talking of death. One of our young professors at Fuller Theological Seminary was facing death from cancer, and we could scarcely talk of anything else.

Bad vibrations are what a lot of people feel when the grim subject of death intrudes. Bishop Fulton Sheen has called death the "great taboo of our society" as sex was the great taboo of Victorian society. Want to spoil a party? Talk of death in loud tones and watch the crowd scatter. It's taboo, a subject that genteel people do not discuss at parties.

In our modern patterns of living, natural death has been removed from the sphere of everyday life. We live longer now, on the average, and far fewer of us die as youngsters or young adults. During the days that Ruth and I lived in Scotland, we often visited old cemeteries, especially the one at the cathedral in St. Andrews. There in the shadow of the gray stone ruins we read the weather-scarred inscriptions on the tombstones. Time after time we noted that families had lost several children in a few days. Whooping cough, diphtheria, smallpox—what dread plague was it that had swept into a fisherman's cottage and robbed him of his young? Medical technology has changed all this, and we are grateful. But the removal of death from everyday life has sharpened our fear of it.

Usually only professionals deal with the dying and the dead. The nurses in our intensive care wards or our convalescent homes, the ambulance drivers and highway patrolmen who flash their lights and sound their sirens at our accidents, the morticians who tend our dead and supervise their funerals shield most of us from direct contact with death. I suppose the vast majority of younger and middle-aged people in our country have never seen a person die.

But more than lack of contact is involved in our fear of death. Death has always been viewed as a harsh intruder. Nineteen centuries ago, a New Testament writer described the human family as "those who through fear of death were subject to lifelong bondage" (Heb. 2:15). This fear of death has prompted witch doctor and wizard, magician and spiritualist to try to dispel it without any notable success.

Modern technology has done little better. We live longer and die more comfortably. But die we do. The death rate in the most healthful of our communities is 100 percent. One might argue that modern technology has strengthened the grip in which the fear of death holds us. Death seems even more terrible today because it is one of the few problems that defy solution. We get bad vibrations from the thought of it because it's a constant and terrible reminder of our finitude. It calls the bluff of boasts of omni-competence. It exposes us as the "frail children of dust, and feeble as frail" that we really are. It brands us as ultimate losers and makes hollow any victories we seem to win along the way.

If the Christian gospel is really going to be good news to the family of man, it just has to deal with death and the terror in which it holds us. Three times in the Gospels we read that Jesus looked death in the eye and stared it into submission. The daughter of Jairus, the son of the widow of Nain, and Lazarus, the brother of Mary and Martha, all knew what it was to hear the voice of Jesus and come alive from the dead. Jesus raised Jairus' daughter minutes after she had died (Mark 5:21–24, 35–43). The son of the widow of Nain was rescued from his own funeral procession (Luke 7:11–17). Lazarus was called from the tomb four days after his death (John 11:17–44). It is his case history that we want to look at more carefully.

THE PROMISE OF FINAL RESURRECTION

When Jesus and his disciples finally arrived in Bethany, the scene was a gloomy one. Lazarus was dead and buried. Mary and Martha were disconsolate, taking whatever faint comfort they could from the condolences of their friends. With Jesus' arrival came some hope, vague and uncertain. "Martha said to Jesus, 'Lord, if you had been here, my brother would not have died. And even now I know that whatever you ask from God, God will give you.'" Jesus wasted no time; he began to give Martha the assurance she looked for: "Your brother will rise again." Devout Jew that she was and faithful follower of Jesus' teaching, Martha answered firmly and in faith: "I know that he will rise again in the resurrection at the last day."

This gave Jesus the opening he wanted. Her faith in what the power of God would do in the future prepared her to hear what Jesus could do in the present. "Jesus said to her, 'I am the resurrection and the life; he who believes in me, though he die, yet shall he live, and whoever lives and believes in me shall never die.' "

This is a magnificent claim. Jesus himself is the resurrection. That great future act of deliverance, when God will re-create the bodies of the human family that have been ravaged by death, when body and spirit so sharply severed by our mortality will be rejoined, is present in Jesus. Tomorrow, with all its hope and promise, is here today in the person of the Man of Galilee.

Resurrection is not just a doctrine about God's power to change the future. Resurrection is embodied in a person—a person who raised the dead and himself was raised from the dead, a person who demonstrated in his ministry and in his own experience that death was no match for him.

The fact that resurrection is personal, that Jesus himself is the resurrection, gives us superb comfort in the midst of our inherent fear of death. Suppose you are in trouble with the law. Perhaps you have been arrested on false charges. You may have some confidence in our legal system, you may take some encouragement from our commitment to due process for every citizen in every circumstance, you may remind yourself that in our tradition of law a man is considered innocent until proven guilty, but none of these doctrines gives you as much assurance as seeing your lawyer walk into the police station prepared personally to see that all your rights are defended. And this is especially true if the lawyer is your friend. His combination of competence in law and commitment to you lifts your fears.

This is exactly what Jesus does to our fear of death.

He tells us that he personally has taken responsibility for its downfall. Even when death seems to have won, as in the case of Lazarus, four days dead, death is done in. Jesus is the resurrection. How we who have seen loved ones walk through death's dark door ahead of us need to know that! How we who feel the daily toll that advancing age takes on us need to remember that!

Jesus is the resurrection. His love and power guarantee the future of all who believe in him. He does not have to head off death. He can deal with it after it has done its worst. His power is so great that it contradicts the wise sayings on which we all were reared: "An ounce of prevention is worth a pound of cure"; "A stitch in time saves nine"; "It does no good to lock the stable door after the horse is stolen." All these proverbs sympathize with Martha's feelings: "Lord, if you had been here, my brother would not have died." "I am the resurrection . . ." Jesus answered; "he who believes in me, though he die, yet shall he live." A lesson of faith is what Jesus wanted to teach. He states this plainly to his disciples on the way to Bethany: "Lazarus is dead; and for your sake I am glad that I was not there, so that you may believe" (John 11:14–15). They could not doubt the reality of the resurrection when they saw Lazarus walk out of his tomb at the Lord's command.

THE PRESENCE OF ETERNAL LIFE

More is involved in Jesus' claim than the promise of future resurrection, so powerfully demonstrated in the case of Lazarus. "I am the resurrection and the life." Where Jesus comes to do his work, eternal life is

127

present—God's own life is revealed. And whenever this happens our lives are changed.

Nothing is so true about our lives as our mortality. Whatever our ethnic background or family history, "mortal" is our middle name. If our genetic background is strong, if we take good care of our health, if God spares us the ruin of war or calamity, we may live a long time. But we are all destined to die. Every headache, cold, or allergy, every twinge and twitch, every muscle spasm or crick in the back is a reminder that we are wearing out.

Yet life does not have to be a long, downhill march toward death. It can be a steady trek toward God, refreshed along the way by the life that Jesus gives right now. Life does not have to be dominated by death and its pressing fear. "Whoever lives and believes in me shall never die." This promise will be literally true for those who trust Christ and are alive on that great day when he comes again to judge the living and the dead. And it is true spiritually for all believers now. Spiritual death, that terrible estrangement from the power and the presence and the love of God, will not happen to us. Jesus is the life, and we are linked to him. Life, not death, is what dominates our living now. And life, not death, is our final destiny.

Not fear of death but faith in Christ is the basic lesson of this story. The purpose of this amazing miracle was not just to create a sensation or to spare the life of a friend. It was to encourage faith: "for your sake I am glad that I was not there, so that you may believe." "Do you believe this?" Jesus asks Martha after he has announced himself as resurrection and life. "Yes, Lord," she answers, "I believe that you are the Christ, the Son of God, he who is coming into the world."

This kind of belief, this wholehearted commitment to who Christ is and what he can do, is exactly what is needed to deal with fear. How do we face our fear of death? By believing, really believing, firmly believing, that Jesus is resurrection and life. For those who belong to him, death may hold twinges of anxiety, but the ultimate terror is gone.

Prayer: Our Father, you have done it again. You have shown us how Jesus speaks to our fears. No wonder your gospel is such good news. Help us to believe it at least as much as we believe the headlines that cry of calamities that rush hundreds into eternity. Help us to trust your Son's word more than we do the daily obituaries which mark the steady march of our friends and neighbors into the life to come. By the hope of resurrection then and true life now, equip us for what history brings our way, including the reality of death. Through Jesus the ultimate winner, we pray.

AMEN.

For further study of related themes refer to the following Scripture passages:

John 1:4; 5:26
John 6:47; 8:51
Revelation 1:18

Your Fear XV
of an Unknown Future

¹⁵ When they had finished breakfast, Jesus said to Simon Peter, "Simon, son of John, do you love me more than these?" He said to him, "Yes, Lord; you know that I love you." He said to him, "Feed my lambs." ¹⁶ A second time he said to him, "Simon, son of John, do you love me?" He said to him, "Yes, Lord; you know that I love you." He said to him, "Tend my sheep." ¹⁷ He said to him the third time, "Simon, son of John, do you love me?" Peter was grieved because he said to him the third time, "Do you love me?" And he said to him, "Lord, you know everything; you know that I love you." Jesus said to him, "Feed my sheep. ¹⁸ Truly, truly, I say to you, when you were young, you girded yourself and walked where you would; but when you are old, you will stretch out your hands, and another will gird you and carry you where you do not wish to go." ¹⁹ (This he said to show by what death he was to glorify God.) And after this he said to him, "Follow me."

²⁰ Peter turned and saw following them the disciple whom Jesus loved, who had lain close to his breast at the supper and had said, "Lord, who is it that is going to betray you?" ²¹ When Peter saw him, he said to Jesus, "Lord, what about this man?" ²² Jesus said to him, "If it is my will that he remain until I come, what is that to you? Follow me!" ²³ The saying spread

abroad among the brethren that this disciple was not to die; yet Jesus did not say to him that he was not to die, but, "If it is my will that he remain until I come, what is that to you?"

—JOHN 21:15–23

Man's imagination sharpens his sense of fear. This great human ability of ours to thrust ourselves forward and anticipate tomorrow's happenings ahead of time makes us highly vulnerable. There's a lot of uncertainty about tomorrow, and that's hard for us to handle.

Robbie Burns, the Scottish poet, saw the issue clearly. He was plowing one day, and his plowshare dug into the carefully built nest of a field mouse. Almost in penance, he wrote a poem, "To a Mouse." You remember the well-known line about "the best laid schemes o' mice an' men" and how they both go wrong. But then Burns went on to say that our human problems are much more painful than the mouse's. To the mouse he says:

> Still thou art blest compared wi' me!
> The present only toucheth thee,
> But, och! I backward cast my e'e
> On prospects drear!
> And forward, though I canna see,
> I guess an' fear.

The anxious present, the haunting past, the fearful future—these are the three tenses by which we conjugate our human verbs. And we can probably make a case for claiming that fear of the future is gripping us all the tighter as life changes ever more rapidly.

Future Shock is what Alvin Toffler called his best-selling book. In some ways it's more frightening than a horror story. It describes the frantic pace of modern life and the toll that change is apt to take on all of us. Confronted by countless varieties of goods, we have to make endless decisions about brand and size and quality and price. We are a society on the move. Every year since 1948, one out of every five Americans has changed his address. We meet more and more people in the moving process and have to cope with new names, new faces, new relationships, new problems. The ratio of the familiar to the strange is changing sharply. New information by the truck load or, perhaps better, the computer load is being dumped upon us. Leaflets, magazines, brochures, pamphlets, paperback books, newspapers threaten to smother us. Information overload, Mr. Toffler calls this, and he warns us that we may actually suffer physically as the result—insomnia, heart palpitations, tension, fatigue.

We need help, help that goes beyond what education and technology can do to cushion us against future shock. Jesus' disciples had their own form of future shock to contend with. From their experience we gain light for ours.

What frightened the disciples was Jesus' talk of leaving them. They had cut their ties with their past to go with him. Their businesses were abandoned; their homes and families left behind. For three years or more their lives had been wrapped in a bundle with Jesus' life.

Where he went, they went. What he commanded, they tried to do. His ministry was their prime concern.

Now he was leaving. And part of his legacy to them was a promise of hostility and persecution in the world. This did nothing to comfort their fears. A conversation between Jesus and Peter brings the problem into sharp focus.

We listen to the conversation just after the famous "Do you love me?" questions, which Jesus concluded with the simple command, "Feed my sheep." Three times Peter affirmed his love of the Master, and three times he was ordered to give himself to the service of the Master's people. What Jesus said next to Peter is the surprise. The blustery fisherman had been restored to fellowship after his night of shame. He who refused to count himself with Jesus' men was singled out for special attention. The restoration was complete.

But Jesus had special plans for Peter, and here is where the surprise comes in. Jesus promised Peter not recognition or reward but death, a special kind of death at that: "Truly, truly, I say to you, when you were young, you girded yourself and walked where you would; but when you are old, you will stretch out your hands, and another will gird you and carry you where you do not wish to go."

THE FEARS WE FACE

To a strong man at the peak of his powers, Jesus promised death. To a valued disciple joyously restored to fellowship, Jesus predicted crucifixion, as the mention of stretching out his hands to be nailed or bound to a cross suggests. The Gospel itself makes clear Jesus' meaning: "(This he said to show by what death he was to glorify God.)"

How did Peter feel? He was confident in his love for Jesus; he was ready to feed his sheep. Then, like a slap in the face, the news of his coming death was handed to him. No use questioning Jesus' word. Long since Peter had learned how trustworthy, how accurate, how infallible Jesus was. And the Master had deliberately introduced his promise with the words of ultimate credibility: verily, verily—truly, truly.

Peter's certainty of the grim news of his coming crucifixion was shadowed with uncertainty. When and how would it come? How much feeding of Christ's flock could he complete before others led him away to his death? What would it be like to die? Would his faith hold firm under pain and persecution?

Even when we know what's going to happen, fear of an unknown future may creep in upon us and begin to work on our insides. No matter how calm we seem to be, the twinges of uncertainty are there. Sometimes they jab us sharply and go away for a while. Sometimes they clutch us tightly and hang on, so that no matter what else we feel they are always there.

Some time ago one of my neighbors calmly packed his bag and walked with his wife about two miles to the hospital near our home. He checked in and went to his room. He did not come home again. He knew he had cancer, a fatal form of it. He had no car, so he walked. He knew to an almost absolute certainty what was going to happen, and he and his wife did all they could to face the inevitable with poise and composure.

Yet even then there was a lot unknown that lurked in their future. A man only dies once, so he can hardly be casual even if he is calm. What about his loved ones? How will they get along? We know that Peter was a married man; his wife's welfare was bound to be on his mind. So was the question about the fate of his friends who also were called to share their faith in the risen Christ.

"Peter turned and saw following them the disciple whom Jesus loved, who had lain close to his breast at the supper and had said, 'Lord, who is it that is going to betray you?' When Peter saw him, he said to Jesus, 'Lord, what about this man?'" John was on Peter's mind. They had been close since the early days of Jesus' ministry. The two of them along with John's brother, James, had been an inner circle, especially close to the Master, the three obvious leaders among the twelve.

Peter's lot was clear: crucifixion. But Jesus had said nothing to anyone else, and Peter was curious, even puzzled. His question was a natural one. Am I the only one of the eleven remaining disciples (remember Judas was dead by now) singled out for this kind of treatment?

Jesus' answer did nothing to ease Peter's puzzlement. "Jesus said to him, 'If it is my will that he remain until I come, what is that to you?'" So indefinite was Jesus' answer that a rumor arose that John was not to die but would live to see Jesus come again.

135

Not only Peter's curiosity was squelched by Jesus' answer, but John's was too. We can be sure that he was concerned about his future. Though he was somewhat younger than Peter, he also had questions about tomorrow and the next day. He had not missed what Jesus had said about tribulation and persecution in the world. But not one ounce of information did Jesus give him about the future.

Peter knew how he would die, yet his certainty was clouded with a lot of uncertainty. John did not know what would happen to him, yet his uncertainty was brightened by a lot of certainty. The risen Lord had broken the back of death and ruined its ability to conquer Christ's people. Love that would die for a sinner and power that could defeat death are an unbeatable combination. Peter in his certainty and John in his uncertainty both knew that.

Sometimes we are well aware of our dying. My neighbor got the message and walked to the hospital. Sometimes we don't have it in mind at all. My father finished a sermon on love, closed his Bible, and dropped dead in the pulpit. Whether the fear we face is the certainty of death or its uncertainty, Jesus' words are directed to our fear.

The Master We Follow

In both parts of the conversation with Peter, fear was neither Jesus' final word nor Peter's final response. When Jesus predicted Peter's death, he concluded the prediction with a brief and powerful command: "And after this he said to him, 'Follow me.' " And when Jesus re fused to comment on John's lot, he snapped the conversation shut with "what is that to you? Follow me!" Not the fears that we face but the Master that we follow should be the center of our concentration.

The future holds nothing beyond his coping. His disciples sensed that. One of their own had betrayed him, yet he did not turn bitter. A cruel political plot had been mounted against him, yet he did not panic. Sharp rejection, extreme pain, death itself were baptized into God's purposes. Everything that men meant for evil God had turned into good. When Jesus said "Follow me," Peter was ready. Temporarily he had gone his own way, and it led to a dead-end street. Now he was ready to follow. The love and power of Christ compelled him. He had to say yes, even though the shadow of his coming cross hung over every step he took.

Even death is glory if it comes from following Christ. Peter knew that. He had heard Jesus speak of his own death as glory. "The hour has come for the Son of man to be glorified. Truly, truly, I say to you, unless a grain of wheat falls into the earth and dies, it remains alone; but if it dies, it bears much fruit" (John 12:23–24). No death, no obedience to the Father; no death, no demonstration of love; no death, no forgiveness for the church. Christ's death was a moment of glory. So was Peter's: "(This he said to show by what death he was to glorify God.)" And so can your death be a moment of glory, if your life's response is to go with Christ.

To his mouse, Robbie Burns confessed: "And forward, though I canna see, I guess an' fear." To his men, Jesus said: "Take heart, it is I; have no fear." When we

137

hear that voice and those words, we can follow anywhere. Even into the unknown future.

> Prayer: Lord, this conversation with Peter hits us all. We know that death awaits, and for some of us it is already in sight. Help us to live life to the full in the face of death by following Jesus. Then lead us to the fullest kind of life beyond death at Jesus' side. In his name we pray.
>
> **AMEN.**

For further study of related themes refer to the following Scripture passages:

Jeremiah 29:11
Lamentations 3:22–23
I Corinthians 15:58

Conclusion

This is a scary subject—fear. Scary because it may revive ghosts of fears long buried. Scary because it may put the spotlight on fears we are trying to ignore. Scary because it may send us searching for fears that do not now exist.

Scary, most of all, because it may lead us to focus on fear itself rather than on Jesus' mastery over it. We may be so seized by the terror on the faces of our fellow disciples in the boat that we fail to hear the voice of the Man who walked on the water. The white knuckles, the fingernails that dig into the palms, the tense neck, the heart in the mouth, the fluttering in the stomach—these we feel, the telltale signals of our fear. Signals that come through so strong that they may blur the words of calm assurance: "Take heart, it is I; have no fear."

But Jesus is as patient as he is powerful. Our lack of faith does not put him off, though he reserves the right to chide us for it. He keeps calling in the night; he keeps walking toward our boats. Persistence was important, he taught us in his parables; and he practiced what he preached. His importunity is our opportunity. If at first we don't hear, he usually calls again. His major goal is not to give us enough rope to hang ourselves, but to throw out the lifeline to draw us to him.

Even our more insistent fears are no match for him. His love will outlast them all. He is much more heavily committed to save us by his love than we are to destroy ourselves by our fears.

Facing our fears, whatever shape they take, is important. If it were not, I would not have written a whole book to urge us to do just that. But facing Jesus Christ is infinitely more important. We must do that whether we fear or not.

We face Jesus Christ, not just as a ladder of escape from the fires of fear but as the road to God, the sole bridge over the gulf of our separation and rebellion. We face Jesus Christ, not just as a gentle man who calms the storms of life but as the mighty Lord, the source of life itself.

We face Jesus Christ, not as the righteous referee who tells us that our fears are out of bounds but as the divine Rescuer who saves us from all the foul things in life we call fair. We face Jesus Christ, not as the carping critic who writes strong copy about our mistakes but as the suffering Savior who died to undo these mistakes. His pardon furnishes forgiveness for all our wrongs, even our fears.

How do we face our fears? By facing our Savior, who is greater than them all.